MODERN COMBAT SHIPS 1

'Leander' Class

Below:
Seen in May 1983 is *Hermione*, a Batch 3 Sea Wolf conversion. *Mike Lennon*

F58

MODERN COMBAT SHIPS 1
'Leander' Class

Cdr C.J. Meyer OBE, RN

LONDON
IAN ALLAN LTD

Contents

Front Cover:
The Royal Navy 'Leander' class frigate HMS _Apollo_ (F70) pictured making a turn while operating in the English Channel during May 1983. _Martin Horseman_

Below:
Scylla, a Batch 3 Gun 'Leander', enters harbour. _RN — Neptune_

First published 1984

ISBN 0 7110 1385 3

Published by Ian Allan Ltd, Shepperton, Surrey; and printed by Ian Allan Printing Ltd at their works at Coombelands in Runnymede, England.

Acknowledgements

Many helped me with the preparation of this book, some knowingly and some with little idea that I would remember their stories and experiences over the years. It is to the latter that I owe the most thanks, perhaps, in the sense that their unprompted enthusiasm for their ships and fellow shipmates is really the inspiration which makes the story worth telling. I am sorry for the many shortcomings and omissions for which I may be responsible in this book and I hope that none will be hurt by them.

I am particularly grateful for the help of many in the Ministry of Defence Navy Department both for helping me find photographs and for allowing me to use them. The photographic sections at HMS *Osprey*, HMS *Excellent*, and HMS *Neptune* proved extremely patient and understanding in assisting with my search.

I would also like to thank the commanding officers of each RN, RAN, RNZN and RNIN 'Leander', all of whom wrote to me in response to what can only have been an unwelcome addition to their paperwork. Likewise, the Indian, Netherlands, New Zealand and Australian naval attaches in London were equally helpful and supplied both material and permission to use it.

The Naval History Branch gave me free rein amongst its facilities (which are extensive) and I am particularly grateful for the encouragement given by Lt-Cdr Mike Wilson as well as the Head of the Branch.

The Editor of the *Navy News* passed material to me. Paul Beaver also passed material and offered to help. Lt David Colyer helped considerably with the engineering details and his willingness to educate me is greatly appreciated.

Lt Mike Davies was kind enough to lend for a protracted period and let me use a personal scrap-book made up by his wife whilst he was serving as a leading radio operator in HMS *Dido*. I hope I have done him justice.

Thanks must also go to Bob Downey for the excellent line drawings.

Finally, my wife, Colette, suffered as much as anybody through this book and, as with all other things, remained a constant and vital source of encouragement.

Cdr C. J. Meyer

Below:
Dido off Gibraltar in June 1973. *RN — Tiger*

Abbreviations

AA	anti-aircraft		MAD	magnetic anomaly detector
AD	air direction		MATCH	manned anti-submarine troop carrying helicopter
ADA	action data automation			
ADAWS	action data automation weapons system		MCM	mine counter measures
			MoD	Ministry of Defence
AI	action information		MV	motor vessel
ANZUK	Australia, New Zealand and United Kingdom		NATO	North Atlantic Treaty Organisation
			RAN	Royal Australian Navy
AS	anti-submarine		RAS	replenishment at sea
ASD	air search and direction		RCN	Royal Canadian Navy
ASH	anti-submarine helicopter		RFA	Royal Fleet Auxiliary
ASM	anti-submarine missile		RN	Royal Navy
ASW	anti-submarine weapon/warfare		RNIN	Royal Netherlands Navy
ATW	ahead-throwing weapon		RNZN	Royal New Zealand Navy
Bn	battalion		SAM	surface-to-air missile
CAAIS	computer assisted action information system		SAR	search and rescue
			SATCOM	satellite communication
DAISY	digital automatic information processing system		SEATO	South-East Asia Treaty Organisation
			SMR	Signal Micromin Reckoner
DASH	drone anti-submarine helicopter		STANAVFORLANT	
DLG	guided missile frigate			Standing Naval Force Atlantic
ECM	electronic counter measures		STWS	shipborne torpedo weapons system
ESM	electronic support measures		TBD	torpedo boat destroyer
EW	electronic warfare/early warning		TS	training ship
GP	general purpose		TT	torpedo tube
HF/DF	high frequency direction finder		USN	United States Navy
IFF	identification friend or foe		VDS	variable-depth sonar
kt	knots			

1 The Need

HMS *Hastings* never went to sea. Indeed, it was never even launched. A Type 12 frigate, it had been redesigned before half complete as the first of a new class of GP frigates and was launched on 22 December 1961 as HMS *Dido*. Even so, it was denied a further title because a sister ship had been commisioned shortly before as HMS *Leander*. Thus the 'Leander' class was born and would become, by 1973, the largest class of major warship in the Royal Navy.

The *Leander* went to sea at a time when memories of World War 2 were still vivid. The ship revived, uncomfortably soon for some, a famous name; cruisers of that class having seen distinguished service during the struggle, had barely been struck from the active list — some were still in commission in Commonwealth navies. Not only did *Leander* appear unlike any cruiser, it did not look like a destroyer (or even a frigate) either. As a Modified Type 12 frigate the ship was claimed as a maid of all work, yet this had always been the duty of destroyers, which it clearly was not. Frigates were not supposed to have such pretension.

It is as well to recall the history of the frigate which, in the early 1960s, may not have been remembered by all. The story is as shifting as the birth of the present-day 'Leanders'.

The term frigate was first used by the French to refer to smaller, lightly-armed ships which were intended to act as observers for ships of the line. Frigates became a standard type of warship and in Britain, like France, were ranked next to the multi-decked ships which formed the line of battle. In the 18th and 19th centuries their exploits became famous — from maintaining the blockade off the lee-shore of northwest France month in and month out, to the dashing individual actions of the American War of Independence and between old rivals in the West Indies. (A yet smaller type of ship in the British Navy was known as the sloop, being approximately equivalent to the French corvette.) With the introduction of steam in the 19th century, and the expansion of the British navy, frigates were developed beyond recognition.

The *Warrior*, a famous ironclad displacing 9,000 tons, was rated as a frigate and it was not until virtually the last decade of the century that the term lapsed, all the former frigates by then being rated as cruisers. On 3 March 1943, 55 years later, the term frigate was used again. On this occasion it was felt appropriate for the 'River' class ships, which were to be enlarged corvette types built on the lines of the escort destroyer. They displaced 1,400 tons — heavier than prewar destroyers — and their achievements were soon to match those of their wooden forebears in both sea-keeping and individual daring. Thenceforward the British frigate category embraced not only the 'Lochs' and the 'Bays' but former sloops of the 'Black Swan' class, corvettes of the 'Castle' class and destroyer escorts of the 'Hunt' class. During World War 2 some 75 British frigates, or ships which would now be classed as frigates, were lost.

By 1945 some bitter lessons had been learned and more were clearly round the corner. The submarine had already developed the ability to

Left:
A 'Leander' is launched — the clean hull-form is striking. *RN — Excellent*

Above:
HMS *Dido* as built, 1963, with Bofors. *Dido* was converted from the Type 12 frigate *Hastings*. *MoD*

remain submerged for prolonged periods and nuclear power was to be a reality within 10 years. The impact of air power at sea had been equally demonstrated and the jet engine was already proven. In an atmosphere of shock at the failure of the second 'Great War' to solve the world's political problems, the prospect of a new war at sea to be waged with weapons of a completely new potential demanded a fresh look at warship design. Hindsight may suggest better political and military solutions than those chosen, but such was the crucible in which the 'Leander' class was formed.

Firstly, it seemed that the need to operate in every ocean of the world was no less important than ever. Above all, the variety of tasks required

of the Royal Navy was increased rather than simplified, for whilst the complexity of maritime operations urged a high degree of specialisation, the dissolution of an empire in circumstances of some delicacy denied the opportunity to ignore any particular threat. The common factor remained the sea, and ships were required which could remain underway in the Far East and North Atlantic. They had to be able to do so in tropical storms and arctic gales without undue loss of fighting efficiency or the risk of damage. The demands of the sea were precisely those that had been made upon Nelson's frigates.

Secondly, the fragility of world peace had inspired the birth of new alliances around the world. Britain belonged to SEATO, CENTO and NATO but it was, perhaps, the strategy of the latter which had the more profound effect on naval thinking. It will be remembered that NATO's response to aggression was to be massive nuclear retaliation on a scale to render thoughts of any adventure against the Alliance self-destructive. Thus the Striking Group became the hub of operations in the event of a major conflict at sea. Whilst no one could predict with any confidence what would happen after the strike, it was clear that a group capable of delivering such a blow would require the most complex weapons systems and communications available at the time and there was a strong body of opinion which suggested that any test of NATO's resolve might easily be made against the trade-routes across the sea. Far from being a remote possibility, a war at sea seemed as likely as ever — and it was likely to be prolonged.

As for the weapon systems which navies had to face it is difficult to place them in any order of importance or ease of solution of the threat. It is not really necessary to try.

The first threat was from high-speed long range aircraft which reduced warning times to a matter of minutes unless the horizon could be dramatically extended. Powerful and bulky radars could achieve this and as a first line of defence friendly aircraft could be directed to intercept an incoming raid at a safe distance from the force. Defence against those raiders able to penetrate further would depend upon ship-borne AA systems that could be brought to bear rapidly and accurately. By the mid-1950s the spectre of guided and ballistic missiles had materialised, reducing warning and reaction times yet further. A well-aimed bofors gun could no longer provide the answer and the development of SAMs was proceeding. The solution was provided in the USA by the Talos-Tartar-Terrier family of missiles and in Britain by Seaslug. The latter, efficient and reliable as it proved to be at the time, required a ship

Above:
The Need — the new class of frigates would have to combat the submarine menace. The small sun is in fact a reflection in the top window of the periscope. *RN — Neptune*

Below:
Ajax in a frigate's proper place? Prior to modernisation the ship is escorting an attack carrier group off East Africa. *RN — Excellent*

Below right:
The Task Force at sea. Two 'Counties' and two 'Leanders' escort Victorious off Aden. *RN — Excellent*

of some 5,000 tons to carry it and its ancillary electronics. A smaller missile was also needed, for close range air defence.

At the same time the performance of submarines had changed beyond recognition. With the greater power now possible using nuclear propulsion it was clear that submarines would be able to operate at very high speed, remain submerged almost indefinitely and thereby outdistance any existing surface ship. In fact the problem was similar in many ways to that of air defence for the solution lay in extending the AS horizon of the surface force. Powerful long range sonars were under development and stand-off AS weapons were likewise being designed. It was not generally realised at the time (and is still often imperfectly understood) that the submarine had its own problems, whether it could go faster or not, for it shared the problems of detection and a stand-off weapon with which to engage its prey. Be that as it may, the alarm at the prospect of such a submarine threat added great momentum to the design of AS weapons systems which demanded space in the ship not only for the hardware but the command and control facilities upon which their effective use depended.

Whilst such sophisticated threats were the subject of much energy and discussion in theorising on the possible turn of events during a major naval war, a quite different series of engagements had been experienced by those at sea. Operations off Korea and Suez revealed that many traditional naval functions were by no means dead, and anti-insurgency operations off Malaya, Cyprus and Palestine had added a new dimension to 'peace-keeping'. None of these events could be ignored.

In 1955 the British Government stated that:

'The Royal Navy requires therefore, carriers operating the latest aircraft; ships armed with guided weapons; escorts capable in co-operation with carrier and shore based air forces of providing protection for our shipping; submarines and amphibious forces; minesweepers to keep the sea lanes clear for vital supplies. All these ships must be well equipped and maintained in a high state of readiness.'

This did not exactly describe the Fleet inherited from World War 2. By 1957 the steady rise in the cost of defence equipment, coupled with the state of Britain's economy, had somewhat limited the size and scope of the 1955 master-plan. After much discussion it was decided to retain the principle of the Task Group built around the carrier and that three operational groups should be maintained; two in Home and Mediterranean waters and one in the Far East. The construction of two classes of frigate had been started during the Korean War; of these 11 had been commissioned, 12 were under construction and a further 21 were on order. This programme was left intact in order to provide the Fleet with a modern AS force.

The 'Leanders' were to form an extension to that force of frigates — and, eventually, its backbone.

2 The Crucible

The need for a new generation of frigates may have been clear enough but ships are not built overnight. In 1960 11 'Lochs' and five 'Bays' were still in service with the Royal Navy as well as others with the Royal New Zealand, Royal Australian and South African navies. The 'Lochs', successors to the 'River' class, were still providing the resident guardship in the Persian Gulf and fond are the memories of their huge reciprocating triple-expansion engines developing 5,500shp with the aid of two Admiralty three-drum boilers. (Some PO stokers who forfeited digits in the service of checking bottom-end bearings may have less fond memories but they are vivid all the same.) Their wood-sheathed decks formed an integral part of their air-conditioning system — no less for those between decks than those obliged to stand on the upper deck in the Arabian sun. The curries provided by Goanese cooks and stewards were renowned throughout the Fleet and these fine ships were instrumental in maintaining stability in a corner of the globe where today's record of peace is less than perfect.

Four 'Bays', themselves developments of the 'Lochs', were completed in the mid-1950s as survey vessels and two served as dispatch vessels on the Far East and Mediterranean stations. Their record during the 15 years after the war was second to none and not confined to flag-showing. Operations off Korea, prolonged periods at sea without base or afloat support, were not achieved by makeshift ships without great skill by the companies of both 'Lochs' and 'Bays'.

But with the best will in the world they could not fit into the Task Group concept. For this task a series of conversions and new construction threw some confusion into the melting pot by introducing type numbers which seemed to avoid any form of logic to the classes in question.

The Type 16 conversion was a limited modernisation applied to 'T', 'O' and 'P' class destroyers transforming them to fast AS frigates. The process did not include complete stripping of the hull and the ships retained the appearance and some of the armament of the standard British destroyer. The conversion had the merit of being rapid, they retained the original torpedo tube mountings and their AA armament was stronger than that of their contemporaries. Fast they most certainly were, developing some 40,000shp through two three-drum type boilers and Parsons geared turbines. They could achieve 34-35kt but provided with two fixed ahead-throwing Squid AS weapons and short range sonar their AS effectiveness was questionable.

Destroyers of the 'Z', 'W', 'V', 'U' and 'R' — plus one 'T' (*Troubridge*) — classes were given the more thorough Type 15 conversion. In fact, they underwent complete reconstruction involving stripping down to deck level, extending the forecastle right aft, erecting new superstructure and mounting new armament. Later ships carried the trainable Limbo AS mortar; all were redesigned to be fought from an operations room and together they represented the postwar British conception of fast AS frigates. Admittedly they had lost a little speed during their conversion for although they retained the same propulsion system as the Type 16 conversions their displacement was increased by some 500 tons to about 2,700-2,880 tons. The last Type 15 conversion was completed in 1957 and in many ways these ships provided the prototype for the new generation — they certainly provided the trials platforms for most of the new frigate weapons systems.

The new construction frigates reflected a continuation in specialisation and were produced in two basic hull forms and were designated 'first' and 'second' rate frigates.

The second raters were confined to the 'Blackwood' single-screw 'utility' AS frigates. Of all-welded prefabricated construction they were lightly armed by any standard except in the matter of two Limbo mountings and medium range sonar. Their propulsion machinery was originally an improved steam turbine system giving 15,000shp and a claimed 28kt. The ships were not comfortable in a seaway and during fishery patrols off Iceland their hulls proved unequal to the task without strengthening. Against all these defects must be set their AS performance in favour of which any submariner of the day would testify. They had a remarkable ability to turn very quickly to the extent that they proved time and time again the submariners' attacking rule that assumes a frigate will instantly turn straight towards a submarine at the very moment the submarine stops looking. That part of the screen occupied by a Type 14, as these ships were officially designated, was not the ideal place to penetrate in search of a carrier.

The 'Cathedrals', officially designated Type 61, were designed as first rate AD frigates. Powered by eight ASR1 (Admiralty Standard Range 1) diesel engines, they were intended to serve in directing both shore-based and carrier-borne aircraft, and as ocean radar pickets. Operating far ahead of the Task Group they required great endurance (provided by their diesels) and were provided with self-protection in the form of a twin 4.5in mounting and two fixed Squid AS mortars. They carried comprehensive ASD radar, of course, and could be used as light destroyers in surface action groups for offensive operations. The hull was all-welded and, like the Type 14s, largely prefabricated to allow rapid building. Displacing 2,330 tons (with the now familiar high bow) their seakeeping qualities left very little to be desired.

Of similar hull-form and diesel propulsion, the 'Cats', or Type 41 AA frigates were built to protect convoys against air attack and, officially, to serve as medium destroyers in offensive operations. Their two twin 4.5in gun mountings and associated fire control equipment provided a broadside second only to the 'Darings' and they shared the Type 61s' endurance and flexibility in maintaining an intact propulsion system. Like the 'Cathedrals' they continued to serve well into the 1970s.

But it was the Type 12 'Whitby' class which found the bulk of the new generation of first rate frigates. Designed as AS frigates they incorporated all the lessons of the Type 14s and were declared as the 'quality' type. Completed from 1956 onwards they proved remarkable in heavy weather with the high forecastle keeping them exceptionally dry. An enclosed bridge with wide vision proved excellent in Arctic waters and the operations room was, at the time, a revelation in modern command and control techniques. Fitted with medium range sonar, two Limbo depth charge mortars and comprehensive communications equipment they very soon proved good AS escorts against all comers. The departure from traditional design was complete in the Type 12, except in the case of propulsion which remained to be provided by two Babcock & Wilcox boilers and geared turbines giving

Below:
The 'Leanders' were the result of the need for a new generation of frigates. This is *Danae* working up speed.
RN — Excellent

Above:
A half-sister and forerunner of the class — *Eastbourne* in Scottish waters, 1968. *COI*

Right:
Should the Type 81s have been the basis for the new design? The 'Tribal' *Tartar* enters the Pool of London soon after reactivation during the Falklands conflict. *Paul Beaver*

30,430shp and a speed of some 30kt. The changes made seem obvious in retrospect, but were less so in the mid-1950s. For example, the very principle of conning a ship from an enclosed bridge, let alone an operations room to all intents and purposes between decks, was the subject of some reservation at the time. There was great debate as to where and who the officer of the watch should be and who was responsible for what. Not that these matters were not easily and quickly solved, it was the change in concept which fertilised imaginations to deal with the rapid onrush of even newer weapons systems.

We know that the Type 12, as modified, was to become the 'Leander', but the background is not complete without a brief look at the GP frigates which closely followed the Type 12s for it has often been suggested that these formed a better basis for extension and modernisation.

The Type 81s ('Tribal' class) were all begun between early 1958 and late 1960, were launched between 1959 and 1962 and the last to be completed joined the Fleet only shortly after *Leander* itself. They were designed to fulfil economically all the various functions of frigates at the expense of an outstanding performance in any one specialised role. It was hinted at the time (by the cynical who were, presumably, those who found the idea of an enclosed bridge difficult to work with) that they were furnished with two funnels not only to emulate their prewar namesakes but to convince Arab dhows that they were faster than the 'Lochs' (which they were, anyway). Wood-sheathed upper decks added credence to speculation about their future employment and indeed they did take over the duties of patrolling the Persian Gulf with no less success than their predecessors.

Fine looking ships displacing 2,300 tons and mounting two conventional, if not to say old-fashioned, single 4.5in guns, they contained many more revolutionary features than the Type 12. Driven by a combined steam and gas turbine (COSAG) powerplant consisting of a single-cylinder steam turbine developing 12,500shp coupled with a 7,500shp gas turbine, they could (and can still) steam at 28kt. What is more they could get underway from cold with virtually no delay, using only the gas turbine. The design and layout of compartments allowed them to operate in nuclear fallout with the propulsion machinery

controlled remotely, and they were the first British ships to be designed to carry a helicopter.

The argument in favour of the Type 81 as a more suitable basis for modernisation has pointed mainly to its propulsion system (which has indeed formed the basis of modern plants in the RN, even if others have been slower to recognise its merits) and to the single 4.5in guns, which might have been replaced by the new Mk 8 4.5in mounting. And so the argument has gone on. This conjecture was of course possible even in the late 1950s/early 1960s but, faced with a hull-form of exceptional quality and a proven propulsion system, time argued strongly for using the early Modified Type 12s ('Rothesay' class) as the basis for development. Not least of all, the insurance provided by two screws appeared to be a highly desirable quality in a ship required to remain on station without shore support.

The die was cast and HMS *Leander* was completed in March 1963. The ship was the prototype of a more versatile group of fast AS frigates and was, in fact, officially described as a GP frigate. Flush from stem to stern, it retained the basic hullform of the 'Rothesays' and their seakeeping qualities, speed and manoeuvrability. A very high standard (for the times) of accommodation was provided for the ship's company with separate dining halls, bunk sleeping and air-conditioning throughout mess decks and operational spaces. A large flightdeck and hangar accommodated a Westland Wasp helicopter and the scene was set for the frigate's entry into the age of computers, satellite communications, guided missiles and an all-volunteer navy.

Below:
The original artist's impression of *Leander*. There seems to be a remarkable resemblance to the 'County' class guided missile destroyers. *RN — Excellent*

Bottom:
***Leander* undergoes contractor's sea trials before delivery — note the Red Ensign. Under these circumstances the ship's company is 'hired' by the contractor.** *MoD*

The Crew and Life Onboard

Left:
A junior rates' mess. Unrecognisable by previous standards but still, of course, basically unchanged since built. *COI*

Below:
The Wardroom — somewhat full. Its inhabitants commonly liken it to a railway carriage. *COI*

Above left:
Geffer (soft drinks) at the NAAFI canteen. 'Leanders', in common with the rest of the Fleet, carry their canteen manager wherever they deploy. *COI*

Left:
The junior rates' dining hall. Food is prepared and cooked in a central galley. *COI*

Above:
The chief petty officers' mess. *COI*

Right:
The helmsman should be steering a proper course and the young chef has a roast dinner ready which can probably be smelled throughout the whole ship.
RN — Leander

3 Construction

'LEANDER: Who would enter for small craft, when the *Leander*, the finest frigate in the world, with a good spar deck overhead to keep you dry, warm and comfortable, and a lower deck like a barn, where you may play leap-frog when the hammocks are up, has still room for 100 active seamen, and a dozen stout lads for Royal Yardsmen? The Officers' cabins are building on the main deck to give every two a double berth below. Lots of leave ashore, dancing and fiddling on board, and four pounds of tobacco served out every month. A few strapping fellows who would eat an enemy alive, are wanted for Admiral's bargemen.'

Thus ran the recruiting advertisement for the second *Leander* in 1814 and if the results it achieved were doubted by the Admiral, who complained that he had never seen so many cripples, criminals and boys congregated in one ship, the general spirit of the claims published could have been applied to the new class of GP frigates launched under *Leander's* class name in the 1960s. The latter were, as we have seen, the result of a great deal of experience gained during the mere 15 years since the conclusion of World War 2 in a wide variety of vessels and the application of much thought towards the needs of modern warfare at sea. They were designed as the most powerful and seaworthy ships ever possessed by the Royal Navy to hunt down and destroy high-speed submarines and to engage other surface units, aircraft and shore targets. It was intended that they should be able to take their place in Task or Escort Groups as well as being powerfully-armed ships suitable for deployment as single units to deal with Cold War tasks at sea.

To these ends, three new features were applied to the Modified Type 12, 'Rothesay' class, hull:

● Long range air-warning radar and improved communications equipment were added to the AI outfit.
● VDS as well as the most up-to-date hull-mounted sonar was installed.
● The upper deck was reshaped to house a Wasp AS helicopter armed with homing torpedoes or depth charges. This required the provision of both flightdeck and hangar.

These basic changes predicated certain improvements in the Type 12 ships' services and, at the same time, every effort was made to include every modern form of ship's fitting that could be placed in ships of their size. Stabilisers were required to permit flight operations over a wider range of weather conditions — and, of course, lessened the engineering problems involved in stabilising other weapons systems. Hydraulic winches were provided for VDS handling, Seacat missile lifts, capstans, boat hoists and helicopter handling gear. The bridge layout was improved to give better all-round visibility and navigation facilities. By no means least, the standard of accommodation provided for the

Below:
Designed to sink upright? *Achilles* **alongside after a collision in dense fog whilst transiting the Dover Strait.** *RN — Excellent*

Right:
The internal compartments of a 'Leander' class frigate.

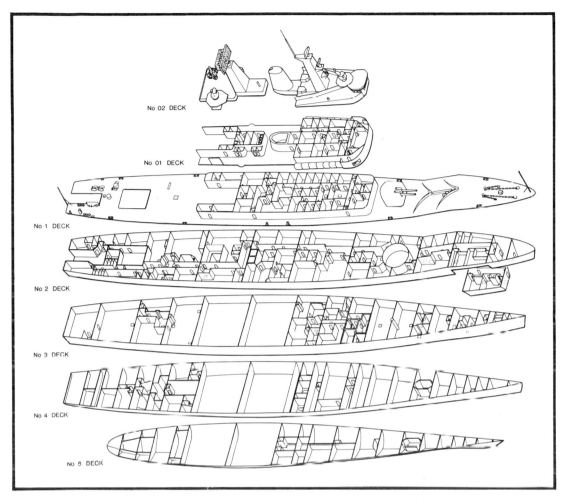

No 02 DECK

No 01 DECK

No 1 DECK

No 2 DECK

No 3 DECK

No 4 DECK

No 5 DECK

ship's company was designed to include bunks for each man, air-conditioning in all living spaces and dining hall messing. Compared with previous warships, the finish applied to bathrooms, passages, offices, mess decks and the upper deck was designed with a view to easy cleaning by the use of Formica and the filling in of awkward corners. Ship husbandry had been made easier as a deliberate policy which ran hand in hand with the requirement to reduce decontamination problems to an absolute minimum in the event of battle in a nuclear, chemical or biological environment. The sub-division of compartments and design of damage control facilities received great attention — to the extent that it has often been claimed by the more enthusiastic damage control experts that the class was 'designed to sink in the upright condition'.

These changes demanded increased electrical power and the opportunity was taken to update propulsion machinery, but that is a subject which deserves its own separate treatment. The result

was a ship, pleasing to the eye, with the following vital statistics:

Length: 372ft
Beam: 41ft
Draught: 13½ft (16ft at the screws)
Displacement: 2,350 tons standard
2,760 tons full load
Machinery: Two Babcock & Wilcox controlled superheat boilers (550lb/sq in at 860°F)
Two shafts, English Electric geared turbines developing 30,000shp
Speed: 30kt
Complement: 19 officers and 245 ratings

The first three ships of the class had originally been laid down as 'Rothesays', so rapid was the implementation of the new design, and from 27 March 1963, when *Leander* was commissioned, until the end of the year a further three ships entered service — *Dido*, *Penelope* and *Ajax*. In the next nine years the total was brought up to

26 in the RN, *Ariadne* being the last to join its
sisters on 10 February 1973. (By then, as a
matter of interest, the ship was the last steam
frigate to join the RN.) Several design changes
had been incorporated into ships as they were
being built or had been added during refits. These
included the 'Broad Beam' version from
Andromeda in 1969 onwards, and so the last 10
ships have a beam of 43ft. By the time *Ariadne*
had joined the Fleet not only had 10 'Leander'
derivatives been completed for foreign navies but
Leander itself had been taken in hand, in December 1972, for mid-life modernisation and conversion. But this is to look too far ahead, for the
time being.

How are these ships outfitted to fulfil their
duties as GP frigates?

Anti-Submarine Warfare

Before looking at the systems and weapons
selected for the 'Leanders' it is as well to reflect
upon the realities of the submarine problem, and
how it was seen to exist, in the 1960s. Submarines had brought Britain dangerously close to
defeat at sea in two world wars and, as we have
seen, by the 1960s submarine design had
reached a point of sophistication beyond, so it
seemed, the advances made in systems designed
for their destruction. 'High speed' meant sub-

marines credited with 30kt for sustained periods,
and 'sustained periods' meant an endurance
beyond that of any surface ship. Not even diesel
submarines regarded the surface as a suitable
environment for their activities; they could sustain
a patrol of six weeks and upwards with only
irregular and short snort-mast exposures to
recharge in gulps of 30min twice a day if they had
been busy. The situation did not look to be
hopeful for the submarine hunters.

Left:
The submarine's nightmare — the frigate's going fast and turning. In fact ships heel out of the turn so this one is turning away to starboard — but to engage with the Mortar Mk 10 or launch the Wasp? . . . Safely past. A rather more comfortable view for the submariner, but to be honest it's a different ship — compare the sea-state, the covered Seacat mounting etc. *RN — Neptune*

Above:
***Leander's* operations room (after modernisation).**
RN — Drake

sonar could then, or now, be compared in any fashion to electro-magnetic radiation and be thought of as a sort of underwater radar. Talk of 'swept' water and 'sanitisation' was, and is, false hope, for the properties of sound in water are affected by a number of variables which are difficult to predict with certainty, although if known they can be measured with precision:

● The speed of sound in water is affected by salinity (density), temperature and pressure to the extent that sound waves are usually bent as differences in these factors cause refraction; sound may be reflected if the change is abrupt and thus bent sharply towards the seabed or trapped in a sound channel, which can be either depressed or near the surface.

● Attenuation of sound in water is not only significant in absolute terms but varies with frequency — the higher the frequency, the greater the attenuation. Unfortunately this phenomenon does not prove to be convenient because the lower the frequency (and therefore the greater the range that may be expected) the less accurate the bearing discrimination.

Note, however, that the submarine experiences the very same conditions so that if it is to gather accurate fire control data it must approach close to its target or rely upon data supplied from another source, be that a homing weapon or a third party in the shape of a shadowing ship or aircraft. In the 1960s no such weapon was at sea although the Soviet Union had developed submarine stand-off missiles which had to be launched from the surface using target information transmitted by data-link from a shadower. So the ASW problem had developed into that of the long range stand-off submarine requiring a different approach to that of the submarine mixing it with escorts. The former called for an integrated effort by aircraft and ships to destroy the data-link and oblige the submarine to surface to delivery its weapon. The latter presented the prospect of a large and thus good reflector of sound obliged to close its target at speeds up to the dramatic sounding 30kt but which break down to a more manageable 1,000yd/min. Solutions to these problems could only be found by imaginative design, but were needed if the 'Leanders' were to prove effective ASW ships.

To deal with the tasks of detection and localisation the class was fitted with HF/DF and high definition surface warning radar as well as communications facilities to allow integrated operations with both long range maritime patrol aircraft and large ASW helicopters. Sonar was, however, to be the main detection and locating device and the most modern available at the time

Yet much had been learned both in terms of AS strategy and tactics as well as the potential offered by technological advances in electronics. Furthermore, enough experience had been gained through submarine exercises in the role of loyal opposition to appreciate that modern submarines were not entirely without their own problems if they were to press home attacks with more than a remote chance of success. The basic problems to be solved remained those of detection, localisation and destruction and they applied to both sides in the contest.

Even before the submarine's evacuation of the surface the properties of sound in water had proved a prime aid to submarine detection. Both active and passive systems had been employed with success although that is not to say that

were fitted. The sonar outfit included sonars for identifying bottomed submarines and an underwater telephone for communications with friendly submarines, but the mainstays of the suite lay in the Type 199 VDS and the hull-mounted Type 184 medium range search and attack sonar.

The Type 199 VDS was designed to overcome the problems of shadow zones created by temperature and density layers by lowering the transducer beneath them and, of course, taking advantage of depressed sound channels in the process. The problems attached to this simple idea are in fact enormous, for not only are the mechanics involved in towing a heavy body at a given depth and relative position to the parent ship complex, the transducer must, in effect, be powered through the towing cable. Canada did much development work during the late 1950s and by 1963 a reliable VDS, in the shape of the Type 199, was in service in the RN so that although the earliest ships were fitted for but not with it, eventually every 'Leander' except *Diomede* was to be so equipped.

The Sonar Type 184, on the other hand, was an entirely British development and incorporated both new ideas and the lessons learned from earlier devices. Its main innovations were the display of doppler effect on returning echoes produced by a moving target, and the use of fixed transmission intervals with a dual frequency system. Cathode ray tube displays were used to improve operator efficiency in target recognition and tracking as well as an all-round and continuous torpedo warning system. The use of doppler effect in this set turned the advantages of a submarine's high speed into one of the most reliable classification clues available to the ASW ship.

It was envisaged that if a submarine were detected at short range it would be attacked with the Mortar Mk 10 (Limbo) depth charge thrower, or, if at long range, by the torpedo-carrying Wasp helicopter. This combination had one immediate effect on design for, in order to provide flightdeck and hangar space for the Wasp, there was room left for only one Limbo mounting as opposed to the two carried in the 'Whitbys' and 'Rothesays'.

The Mortar Mk 10 is a direct descendant of the

Squid ATW from which it was developed in the early 1950s. It comprises three barrels which are trained and elevated together to fire a pattern of three projectiles out to ranges of 2,000yd in any direction save those combinations of range and bearing wooded by superstructure. Range is further adjusted by selecting reduced or increased propellant charges and the projectiles are muzzle-loaded from a protected handling room. With depth settings applied, the mortar is then automatically aimed and fired by sonar and half a ton of explosive is laid in a three-dimensional salvo about the target. Three such salvoes can be fired per minute, each one covering approximately

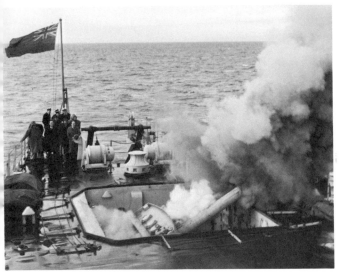

Above:
Leander fires the Limbo three-barrelled AS mortar during contractor's sea trials. *MoD*

Above right:
Firing the mortar locally. *RN — Excellent*

85sq yd within which a submarine would suffer severe damage.

The Wasp helicopter was carried to provide the stand-off weapons system. The use of a torpedo-carrying aircraft was not in itself new for the USN had already selected a drone anti-submarine helicopter (DASH) for its escorts but some original thinking was required to design a manned helicopter for small-ship operations. The decision to take this path has been of incalculable influence on the conduct of naval operations of all kinds and was made easier by the appearance of the Westland Wasp AS Mk 1. This versatile helicopter was given a fully castorable under-carriage for deck operations in heavy weather, a feature no less remarkable because of its simplicity. A single Bristol Siddeley Nimbus turbo-shaft engine was mounted in such a way as to permit easy access for maintenance and changes and, developing just over 700shp, gave a cruising speed of 110kt over a range of some 300 miles with an all-up weight of 5,500lb. In its main role as an AS helicopter the Wasp was to be flown off (if not already airborne) and directed to the sub-marine by a controller in the ship's operations room, there to drop its homing torpedoes. Crewed by one officer pilot, who also commanded the ship's 'flight' of maintenance men, the helicopter was kept at various alert stages for operations. As experience at sea was gained various refinements were made, the most notable being a flightdeck

lighting system, not unlike the deck-landing mirror system in carriers, which permitted flying in a greater range of weather conditions. With room for four passengers and a powered hoist, the Wasp was soon found active on duties in dispatch services and SAR missions.

The original weapon carried by the Wasp, apart from depth charges of varying complexity, was the Mk 44 homing torpedo, later replaced by the Mk 46 version. Both weapons are propelled by electric motor, and were designed for delivery by aircraft, rocket or shipborne Mk 32 torpedo tubes. Various run patterns may be set, depending on the delivery system used, but in the case of the airdrop by Wasp the torpedoes are set by cable to a short enabling run, then to circle in search of the target by active or passive sonar and, finally, to lock on and home on to the submarine. The Mk 46 is deeper diving and faster than the Mk 44 and has a number of improvements in its homing and searching system. The torpedo is designed to strike the target and detonate on impact or may be fitted with a magnetic pistol. The Wasp carries two torpedoes.

One final shot in the class ASW locker must be mentioned. A large winch was fitted aft for towing the Type 182 decoy which seduces submarine-launched homing torpedoes by generating noise which is preferred by the torpedo to that radiated by the ship. This under-water jamming is not ineffective in terms of con-fusing the submarine's own sonar picture by masking the ship's signature, but that is not its primary purpose.

Surface Warfare

The main gun armament fitted to all 'Leanders' on building consisted of twin 4.5in guns mounted on

Above:
Jupiter's flightdeck about to get a wash. There are 'not under control' balls hoisted at the yardarm.
RN — Excellent

Left:
Charybdis's Wasp launching for a MATCH attack; it has the Mk 44 torpedo underslung. *RN — Excellent*

Below left:
A closer view of the Mk 44 A6 torpedo. *RN — Excellent*

the forecastle, controlled by the MRS3 fire control director on the bridge and supplemented by Type 993 warning radar. This was a well-tried combination having been widely fitted in other ships for a number of years.

The Mk 6 twin 4.5in mounting first appeared in the 'Daring' class shortly after the war and could reasonably be described as the product of wartime experience. The armoured turret weighs 45 tons and is mounted on a barbette. The loading cycle is power-assisted with shell and cartridge hoisted from their separate handling rooms below. They are loaded on to a loading tray in the turret and power rammed into the gun breech. The turret is power-operated remotely in primary control but can also be locally operated in both power and hand control. With a maximum range of 10 miles, these guns are very accurate and produce a reasonably rapid rate of fire at 20 rounds per barrel per minute. Put another way, the mounting will deliver over one ton of high explosive and steel in a minute.

The MRS3 fire control system and associated Type 903 radar were also developed before the 'Leanders' although over the years a large number of modifications have been applied. The director is not in itself stabilised but the system as a whole

is gyro-stabilised. The target can be acquired by radar or visually and subsequently tracked in either mode in remote or local control. A control consul and analogue predictor solve the fire control problem and the appropriate corrections are transmitted to the guns. Several versions of this system have been fitted to the class.

While the distinctive sawn-off 'cheese' aerial of the Type 993 radar could be seen at the foremast of every ship, other parts of the surface weapons outfit were either not quite so obvious, or appeared on only some ships. 20mm Oerlikon guns appeared on the superstructure just aft of the bridge on a few ships when they were deployed to the Far East for patrol duties, thus providing a weapon of more suitable proportion to the task in hand. Rocket launchers appeared either side of the boat deck from about 1968 and although their prime purpose was to launch 'chaff' to jam hostile radars, particularly those of anit-ship missiles, they provided the ability to launch rockets for target illumination during night actions without the need to use star shell.

One system which may have been less obvious received great attention, prompted by the need to fill the gap in defence against missile-firing fast patrol craft and shadowers transmitting target data to a lurking submarine. This was the ubiquitous Wasp, fitted with the AS12 wire-guided missile during the late 1960s. The AS12, a short range, solid-fuel missile, was not intended to inflict lethal damage but to cause sufficient

devastation to a target's aerials that it would be unable to continue its activity effectively. Despite the missile's short range it was considered to be an effective weapon to be launched and then guided from outside the optimum range of most close range AA systems of the time. The Wasps of No 829 Squadron had won a new and important role.

Anti-Air Warfare

It will already be obvious that the surface weapons of the 'Leanders' class filled a dual role and they were designed as an AA system from the outset. With the addition of two single Mk 9 40mm Bofors close range AA guns mounted on top of the hangar, this outfit did in fact provide AA defence for the early 'Leanders'. Not that the need for a more effective system had been ignored but none was ready and the first seven ships of the class were commissioned in anticipation of

improvement. *Naiad* was the first to be armed with the Short Seacat AA missile, which has since undergone many modifications and been added to the earlier ships.

Early warning of approaching air-raids was to be provided by the Type 965 long range, air search radar. Mounted on the mainmast, the aerial consists of eight dipoles backed by a wire mesh reflector and, scanning at a relatively low rate, is reminiscent of a key rotating as clockwork unwinds. The is a high-power radar and for this reason a complex series of filters is fitted to minimise interference with communication systems. It is used to plot and track incoming aircraft and subsequently designate targets for the appropriate weapons system. To assist in contact identification one of the various marks of IFF interrogators is fitted, normally mounted on top of the aerial.

Right:
'Leander' foremast. This shows the typical aerial and radar fit of a Gun 'Leander'. A — Type 978 navigation radar; B — UHF aerial; C — VHF aerial; D — Wind direction indicator; E — HF whip aerial; F — Telemetry; G — Type 993 radar; H — HF/DF; I — ESM; J — Wind speed indicator; K — Type 965 radar (mainmast); L — MRS fire control radar. *RN — Excellent*

Below:
Not the most sophisticated of weapon systems, but not to be ignored by the gun-running sampan — the 20mm gun. *MoD*

The Seacat missile system was designed and developed in the 1950s to deal with fast aircraft at close range. Originally conceived as a visually aimed, radio-controlled system it has undergone extensive modification since it was first accepted into service and several versions are now at sea. The system comprises a launcher — a single quadruple mounting being fitted at first — and a director fitted with binocular sights through which the aimer tracks the target using a joystick to transmit radio commands to the missile and thus intercept the target. To this has been added Type 904 tracking radar, as used in the MRS3 gunnery fire control system, to form the GWS22 series of control systems. Later modifications include Marconi TV guidance equipment, usually mounted on top of the Type 904 dish on the director, and, by suppressing 'down' commands once the missile has descended to about 6ft above the sea, a surface-to-surface capability has been added. The missile itself is a small, solid-fuel propelled rocket which carries a relatively heavy warhead, triggered by either a proximity or impact fuse. Mainly because its simplicity has been combined with excellent results in service, the system has proved extremely cost-effective and flexible. One aspect of the system, not forgotten by those directly involved but rarely publicised, was the rigorous selection of the Seacat aimers. The task required the very special skills of good eyesight and quick reactions under extreme pressure as the operator sat in a lightly protected director

Left:
The Seacat AA missile system — director and launcher. *RN — Excellent*

Below left:
Loading Seacat. *RN Excellent*

Below:
Three down, one to go. *RN — Excellent*

eyeball-to-eyeball with a supersonic aircraft. Not every man could remain completely calm in these conditions and although the provision of TV guidance enables the aimer to be rather more accurate in later systems, the 'Seacat Aimer' qualification is hard earned.

Action Information

These weapons systems were fused into a composite, up-to-the-minute picture for the command in the operations room on 'two' deck. Automatic data handling systems were not available in the early 1960s but nonetheless some innovative methods of plot compilation and presentation were used in designing the layout of the compartment. The radar and sonar picture is transmitted automatically and fire control centralised so that with hand filtering all the information upon which to base tactical decisions is immediately at hand. World wide on-line communications have been provided to allow the ship to operate in close company or on its own. The class was designed to be fought from the operations room and thus the break with dodging the elements on the bridge was made complete.

Above:
Action Information in the days of the grease pencil.
RN — Excellent

The Ubiquitous Wasp

Below:
***Ajax's* Wasp lifts a crew member from a British 'O' class submarine near Portland in 1978.** *MoD*

Above:

Lt The Prince of Wales launches *Jupiter's* **Wasp (piloted by Lt L. C. Hopkins) as the ship returns to Devonport in 1974.** *MoD*

Arethusa **under difficult conditions. Note that the Wasp (and men) are able to use the flightdeck in what is clearly a rising sea.** *MoD*

Above:
A movie transfer at sea. *Ariadne's* man seems anxious to see what's on offer — a frequent, and most welcome, event on Beira Patrol when the time came to refuel from the RFA. *RN — Neptune*

Right:
The pilot's view on approach. In fact the helicopter is a Sea King of No 824 Squadron flying out of RNAS Culdrose passing down the side of *Galatea*. *RN — CINCFLEET*

4 The Far East in the 1960s

Message from the Commander, Far East Fleet, to HMS *Dido*:

'Goodbye. I wish you a safe voyage home and a good leave at the end. We shall miss you in this Fleet but you leave in the knowledge that you have done a splendid job in a common effort which has again shown that there is nothing the Navy cannot do.'

During the 1960s 'Leanders' served for long periods with the Far East Fleet and, in common with other ships on that station, were called upon to perform duties as wide ranging as any in naval history. They encompassed the tedious, the

dangerous and the politically sensitive. True, there were 'runs ashore' which spanned every shade of cultural content but, as has always been the way, they spent most of their time at sea waiting for the unexpected. They were frequently rewarded.

It would be impossible to relate the adventures of every 'Leander' for, apart from any other reason, many incidents have now passed into the deepest corners of newspaper cutting files and

Below:
A fine day in the southern seas. *Ajax* has just put the wheel to starboard to follow in the Australian's wake.
RN — Excellent

only a few clues can be gleaned from the stark data of ships' navigation records. The eighth *Ajax*, for example, served continuously in the Far East Fleet from 1964 to 1968, taking an active part in the Indonesian confrontation and covering the withdrawal of British forces from Aden. Even the briefest outline of the ship's activities during those first four years of its life illustrate the variety of situations in which it found itself.

Built by Cammell Laird's at Birkenhead, *Ajax* was commissioned on 11 December 1963 and no sooner had it sailed for sea trials than the next day it successfully salvaged the Spanish freighter *Llusanes* in difficulty off the Casquets. By June the ship had completed testing and tuning, which had been punctuated by a SAR operation for a crashed Seahawk in the Channel, and sailed for Malta and the Far East, arriving in Singapore on 1 July 1964. Within 15 days the ship was on patrol off northeast Borneo, an activity which was to occupy it for the remainder of the year with only short breaks in Hong Kong and Bankok. *Ajax* was back on patrol in early 1965, this time relieved by a cruise to Japan, and was recommissioned on 13 July 1965 for foreign service on the Far East station. It was refitted in Singapore dockyard from October 1965 until February 1966.

During 1965 *Ajax* acted as escort for *Albion*, visited Manila, Hong Kong and Kuching and became a familiar sight back on patrol. In the spring of 1967 it was escorting *Victorious* and spent long periods operating out of Hong Kong and in the Inland Sea. Returning to Singapore in July, the navigator notes that he took his station leave in Port Dixon and Fraser Hill whilst the ship was maintaining but he was soon back at sea in time for the typhoon season off Hong Kong in August. By November *Ajax* was off Aden and involved in support operations until taking up patrol off Beira where it remained with breaks at Mombasa until February 1968. *Ajax* returned to Chatham via Simonstown, St Helena and Gibraltar in March and on 2 April was recommissioned for general service. Since building *Ajax* had steamed 179,367 miles.

Dido's story begins in the same dockyard in April 1965, about to recommission for general service. Ships in any dockyard are not at their best and so it is no particular offence to Chatham to sympathise with the ship's company tripping over air hoses and splashing through muddy puddles as they joined their home for the next two years to find it being powered by a coal-fired donkey-boiler on the jetty. There was little time for them to square away and settle down in their 'high standard of accommodation' before presenting their ship for a second commission. With cleaning, scrubbing and painting things

were, of course, sorted out and in May Capt T. W. Stocker RN read the Commissioning Warrant to the ship's company. The White Ensign was hoisted, the Commissioning Pendant broken out and the captain addressed the 'Didos' before calling upon them to ask for God's blessing using the ancient Gaelic blessing:

'Seeing that in the course of our duty we are set in the midst of many and great dangers and that we cannot be faithful to the high trust placed in us without the help of Almighty God, let us unite our prayers in seeking His Blessing upon this ship and all who serve in her, that she may sail under God's good providence and protection, and that there may never be lacking men well-qualified to offer in her their work and skill for His Greater Glory, and for the protection of our realm and dominions.'

Below:
There are clues to identify this 'Leander'. It's pre-Seacat and the flightdeck code begins with 'E'. It must be *Euryalus*. *RN — Excellent*

Right:
***Hermione,* one of the early Broad Beam 'Leanders'.** *RN — Excellent*

From this moment the wives, children, mothers, fathers and sweethearts watching this time-honoured ceremony could expect to share their men-folk with a ship with 16 battle honours from Toulon, 1793, to Arctic, 1944. *Dido* was soon working up at Portland where the regimen is conducted under the three Fs — fire, flood and famine — and there is no reason to supose that it was not without some relief that submarine exercises, gunnery drills, replenishment operations and every conceivable evolution dispensed with, *Dido* was declared ready to join the Fleet and proceed to its first duty.

Operation 'Jack Tar' involved bringing the Navy to the people, and visits to Hull, Newcastle, Belfast and Liverpool drew a total of 36,312 visitors on board. There were compensations for the hard work this involved for these ports are all loved by the Navy and their hospitality is renowned. No doubt the Clyde Royal Review in August 1965 tested the crew's imagination in a somewhat different fashion but it was clearly a high point in the commission. It would appear that the display of the sort of jobs required of a modern sailor not only proved extremely popular with the Royal Family but was widely reported in the Press. It was said at the time that one chief petty officer, dessed as a pirate (to demonstrate, presumably, the traditional garb for children's parties during port visits) received so much fan mail that he was obliged to grow a real beard to replace the 'Royal' false one to preserve his image.

But time on the Home station was running out. Heading south and east away from the cold European winter at 20kt *Dido* made passage via Gibraltar, Malta and the Suez Canal to the Red Sea. White tropical uniforms appeared and all seemed set for Christmas in Singapore. That is until arrival in Aden when *Dido* was ordered to join *Eagle* and *Salisbury* in patrolling the East African coast and approaches to Aden. This presence had been brought about by the Rhodesian crisis and was soon to provide *Dido* with a situation which demanded no small application of tact.

As a result of sanctions imposed upon Rhodesia, oil supplies to Zambia were being maintained by air. By early December the airlift was in danger of being halted through lack of oil drums in Ndola and so in order to save the situation it was decided to replenish stocks by sending empty drums through Dar-es-Salaam in Tanzania. *Dido* was dispatched from Aden with 70 RAF airlift personnel embarked and a cargo of 250 empty oil drums stowed on the flightdeck; it arrived to find a complex political situation. Following the ship's arrival Tanzania announced that the presence of British servicemen would not be acceptable following a diplomatic break with

Britain. Hardly the same welcome of such recent memories in home waters, and not made better by local rumours that in every oil drum lurked a Royal Marine. One report speaks volumes in stating simply that *Dido* put swiftly to sea after discharging the oil drums.

Christmas in Mombasa and then back to sea escorting *Eagle* in the New Year seemed to indicate a return to more mundane affairs. Christmas had been enlivened by the members of 3F mess in an exchange of seasonal greetings with the current First Secretary of State, George Brown.

From 3F Mess: Hope you have a happy Christmas and we have a prosperous New Year.
From George Brown: Message received, message understood, message reciprocated. All the best. George Brown.

Whether the radio operators of 3F mess knew it or not their concern for prosperity was shared by others at sea as they were soon to discover.

During the weekend of 15/16 January 1966 the sailors who had made the Queen laugh when they were dressed as a pirate boarding party at the Royal Clyde Review were called to assist the master of the British steamship *Sudbury Hill* some 80 miles east of Aden. The Chinese crew, it seems, were unhappy over a pay dispute. With at least one of their number willing to demonstrate skill with an axe, they had offered violence to the master and first mate who promptly radioed for

help. *Dido* proceeded to intercept and sent away a boarding party armed with Bren guns to restore order. A MoD spokesman stated that the mutiny was quelled 'very quickly' without firing a shot. *Dido* returned to Aden and the *Sudbury Hill*, bound from India to Constanta, Romania, with a cargo of iron ore, sailed on to its next port of call, Djibouti.

Aden, it was reported, absorbed 12,000 South Arabian dinars from the ships' companies of *Eagle*, *Blackpool* and *Dido* in what was described as a shopping spree. In the course of much socialising with the garrison *Dido* offered to take a party of soldiers to sea for the day as a break from the arid atmosphere ashore. It being a little choppy on leaving harbour not all the visitors felt able to enjoy their day to the full and it is said that one unfortunate was unable to prevent physical manifestation of his discomfort in the rum tub — fortunately in time to conduct thorough cleansing before 'up spirits' was piped. Reaction on board at such an act of desecration was to compare the lapse with kicking the regimental mascot.

Patrolling the East African coast to enforce sanctions against Rhodesia — which became known as the 'Beira Patrol' — was a monotonous and, at times, difficult task calling for a great deal

Right.
The signal projector is used not only as a searchlight for identifying small boats or searching for survivors in the water on a dark night. RO1(T) Stephenson can flash a message very quickly in a 'hostile electronic environment'. *RN — Drake*

Below:
***Dido* was particularly busy in the Far East in the 1960s — this seems to be one of the ship's quieter moments off Sydney, Australia.** *MoD*

Above:
***Arethusa* floodlit during a port visit in the Far East. The ships in the background make an interesting puzzle — could the carrier berthed astern be HMAS *Melbourne*?.** *RN — Excellent*

of patient work plotting the passage of shipping and identifying their purpose. The success of the patrol in naval, as opposed to political, terms hung upon the determination of every member of the ship's company to maintain the highest standards of efficiency for there was no handy base to slip into for effecting repairs. The young lieutenant in charge of the boarding party could be called upon to make the most delicate decisions in the full glare of international politics and presented a very different prospect to that of the *Sudbury Hill* incident. It was a difficult situation for everybody involved and one for which there was never a clear winner or loser at sea. So it ever was, and no sailor would expect otherwise, although he may wish for more definitive action. The job simply had to be done and for all its tedium (or perhaps because of it) was no less demanding than others warships may be invited to undertake.

Before finally making passage to Singapore, *Dido* was called upon to ferry the Assistant Political Advisor to the Sultan of Mukalla, and his retinue and baggage, to the island of Socotra. A few Wasp loads and whaler trips helped disembarkation and *Dido* turned eastwards and to more patrol duties in the Malacca and Singapore Straits and off Tawau (northwest Borneo), this time in less complex political circumstances and looking for smaller fry than sanction-breaking supertankers.

Patrols in these waters were conducted mainly at night to catch infiltrators and gun-runners using small fishing boats. Not all were particularly friendly when caught and used many ploys to avoid just such an event. It must be a source of some wonder that young men reared in the cool pleasantness of Britain should find themselves searching seemingly innocent fishing boats with no more hostile an appearance than that presented by the old men and small boys who manned them. These events took place in one of the busier shipping routes of the world and many was the darkened frigate called up by passing merchantmen who, having spotted the ship trying to hide in the tropical moonlight, flashed the letter 'P' by signal lamp — 'your lights are out or burning badly'. There was a great deal more to these patrols than searching small boats, for no matter how efficiently the net was drawn at sea the freedom of Sarawak, Brunei and Sabah could not be manufactured by force.

Dido played its part in this 'hearts and minds' campaign by providing its own 'Flying Doctor and

fashion when *Dido* joined exercise 'Sea Imp', a SEATO naval exercise ranging from Manilla to Bankok through which area Typhoon *Judy* passed to add realism. The basic aim of the exercise, apart from working the ships of six nations together, was to exercise the protection of shipping to which end *Dido* led three USN destroyers in a squadron soon to be nicknamed the 'Moonlight Squadron' due to their spirited conduct of night attacks in the role of loyal opposition. Despite the use of radar and modern communications systems the coordination of night attacks requires all the fine judgement known to earlier generations — indeed, those aids are virtually denied the attacker for fear of recognition and thus alerting the defender. The work-up at Portland must have been called to mind with a vengeance during these operations which were agreed by all to have been remarkably successful.

By August 1965 and having been inspected *Dido* was due to return to the Home Fleet. The ship had steamed 68,500 miles at an average speed of $16\frac{1}{4}$kt and enjoyed visits to Hong Kong and Olongopo, Mombasa and Bangkok. There had been the excitement of night exercises, the novelty of quelling a mutiny, the achievement of providing a jungle medical service and a taste of African politics. There were still five months of the commission left, which included a major NATO exercise in the storm-lashed Atlantic and visits to Liverpool (renewing links with the town of Bolton) and Hamburg before paying off in Chatham in January 1967.

Dido's second commission, the crew would most certainly agree, was no more or less demanding than those of other 'Leanders' at the time and whilst we should permit them to argue that they did better than their sister-ships, they would again agree that it was the duller aspects which must not be forgotten. Several months escorting a carrier off the East African coast called for constant attention and quick reaction, as had the long months on patrol off Borneo and Singapore. These required just as much, if not more, effort to ensure that the job was done properly. They demanded just as much reliability and flexibility of the ship itself.

Dentist Service' whilst off Tawau. The Wasp was used to fly the medical officer to deal with cases in the small communities spread over the 2,000 square miles of Sabah. The helicopter flown by Lt Goodman was put down on beaches, in back gardens and jungle clearings to allow Surgeon Lt Bush to set up makeshift surgeries. He and Leading Medical Assistant Rowe dealt with more than 150 patients. Cases of malaria as well as lesser ailments were presented and teeth extractions under the watchful eyes of numerous spectators were described as 'popular'. This service was provided in isolated villages on islands and close to the Indonesian border where the risk of attack was always present. Another job undertaken without fuss but with great skill, it made a tangible contribution to stability in South-East Asia. Meanwhile the ship remained on patrol with guncrews closed up ready for action.

The routine was broken by occasional calls at Singapore and friendly beaches for 'banyan' parties ashore. It was broken in a less relaxing

Replenishment at Sea

For any unit, be it a Task Force or private ship, to operate for any length of time away from shore bases it must be replenished at sea. RAS covers liquids, solids (stores and ammunition) and people. It can be achieved between specialist tankers and stores ships and the recipient; bigger men-of-war transfer to their smaller escorts; and, not least, the helicopter can be used for transfers and can itself be in-flight refuelled. 'Leanders' are no strangers to RAS.

Above all, the evolution must be accomplished in short order for during the process the ships or aircraft concerned are almost literally tied to each other steering a steady course at a steady speed — easy prey to air and submarine attack. There are other good reasons for speed; two ships steaming close aboard feel the effects of each others wakes which produce suction and pressure areas between them. On approaching and disengaging it is to advantage to traverse these areas of mutual attraction or repulsion at some speed in order to not prolong the moment of danger and also to have the control bestowed by reasonable speed through the water. Once 'alongside' a neat state of equilibrium exists with the pressure areas at the bow and stern balancing the suction area amidships. It is no less important to be able to disengage in a hurry.

Solids and people are transferred by jackstay, either heavy or light, on which the load is slung from a block (the traveller) hauled along the jackstay. Liquids are transferred either with the ships steaming abreast or ahead and astern, hoses being rigged between the two. The astern method uses buoyant hose, requires less specialised gear in the supply tanker but is slow and somewhat ponderous. Refuelling abeam requires the tanker to provide special derricks or cranes to support the hoses as they are slung between the ships; it is quicker to connect, quicker to disconnect and, of course can be conducted at the same time as a jackstay transfer.

It is somewhat interesting to note that the Soviet Navy long favoured astern refuelling for which 'standard' merchant tankers require little modification. In common with other Western navies 'Leanders' have remained at sea for prolonged periods by replenishing using mainly the abeam method.

The sequence is standard and well practiced. Generally speaking a down-sea course is selected to provide steadier and drier decks for the crew to work on. A speed of about 15kt gives the 'Leander' good control (less than 8kt is not comfortable). The recipient will approach from the quarter — although a gradual approach from abeam is sometimes better for big ships — and on achieving station the supplying ship fires a gun line across to which is attached a heavier line, the 'messenger', to enable hoses, jackstay, distance lines and telephone lines to be hauled across. Once contact is firmly established it is quite normal for the navigator to adjust engine speed to maintain station whilst the captain watches the distance line, suitable marked with colour lights or flags, to maintain course and distance apart.

Below:
Achilles takes fuel from a carrier. Carriers normally replenish on their starboard side, whether supplying or receiving, so that operations can be seen from the bridge (and in years gone by, to avoid the angle deck). Presumably *Achilles* is not the only customer. *RN*

Right:
Minerva conducts a transfer in the far east — the staff officer even has a white tropical issue bag! Note the officer giving hand signals to the other ship for hauling across and the rating at the ready to slip the gear.
RN — Excellent

Below:
Vertical Replenishment — Vertrep. A Wessex drops stores on the forecastle of **Minerva.** The batsman stands right forward but otherwise there is less evidence of the ship's company. The helicopter pilot would ideally prefer a transfer position where he can easily watch a part of the ship to give him a good reference point. Here he has to look over his shoulder. *RN — Excellent*

Bottom:
Blue Rover fuels **Achilles** in the Northwest Approaches. The distance line runs forward of the hoses and the telephone line is connected amidships. Note the matting to prevent chafing the hoses over **Achilles'** deck.
RN — Neptune

Above:
Danae has just taken station alongside the carrier for
RAS. The gun line is about to be fired across to her and
it will be noted that the strangely deserted appearance
of the upper deck is a standard precaution against injury
from the bolt to which the fine nylon 'coston gun line' is
attached. There are hands ready on the flight deck.
RN — Excellent

Left:
Euryalus takes a jackstay transfer forward. Note the
marker flag on the starboard bridge wing (green for
stores ammunition and people), the human team hauling
the jackstay to tension it (safer than machinery).
Meanwhile the in and out-hauls attached to the traveller
are rove to capstains. *MoD*

Unpleasant results can be achieved if the course chosen is similar to engine revolutions to maintain speed (say, 100rpm on course 100) and the quartermaster transposes engine for course orders. A story has been told of the navigator who looked up to find his captain in the eyes of the ship filming the evolution!

But the standard is high. Replenishment is regularly and safely conducted at 20kt and 'Leanders' have refuelled abeam in a full North Atlantic gale by steaming downwind at 10kt to avoid the very real danger of surfing.

Left:
Arethusa refuels. The sea does not appear to be particularly rough but the ships are close and the interaction of their wake is obvious — certainly it is to those manning **Arethusa's** upper deck. *MoD*

Below left:
Tidespring fuels **Eagle** and **Ajax**. Whilst **Eagle** already has two hoses connected **Ajax** has just got into station, the messenger has been passed and the hoses have been swung out from the tanker. *RN — Excellent*

Right:
A **Wessex III** refuels from **Ajax**. Note the hoist at the port yardarm which signifies that **Ajax** is unable to manoeuvre with freedom. The hoist at the starboard yard is the international call-sign. *RN — Osprey*

Below:
An impressive shot as six ships refuel off Hong Kong. Left to right: **Retainer, Galatea, Reliant, Hermes** (configured as an attack carrier), **Tideflow** and **Minerva**. *MoD*

5 Non British 'Leanders'

Three nations — Australia, India and the Netherlands — chose in the early/mid-1960s to adopt the basic 'Leander' design for new construction programmes. Each had very different defence and naval requirements, but, seeing the advantages of a hull-form proven by British experience across the world, they felt that it was suitable to house their own selection of weapons, sensors and accommodation. Both Australia and the Netherlands had developed their own systems and each had frigate experience in their navies.

The 'Rivers', 'Nilgiris' and 'van Speijks' provide interesting variations on a theme, not least because the observer can hardly fail to notice that each has characteristics in common with the others but not their British cousins. Unmistakably different, they have however provided for the needs of their individual navies with uniform reliability and have demonstrated their ability to meet a wider range of challenges than faced by any one navy. Of no less interest is the very early indication of adaptability which they provided to other 'Leander' owners who have not been above learning from their example.

Netherlands' 'Van Speijks'

By a royal decree of 11 February 1831 it was declared that there should always be a ship in the Royal Netherlands Navy to bear the name *Van Speijk*. It is currently borne by the name-ship of the Dutch 'Leanders'.

The RNIN is called upon by national policy to protect the Dutch coast, the overseas parts of the kingdom in the Caribbean Sea and South America and in any part of the world where Dutch interests are threatened — and Dutch maritime interests are considerable. The Netherlands considers that one of the most important tasks of its navy is to secure the free and unlimited use of the oceans -and a safe passage to the harbours of the Netherlands. To this end the Task Group conept is favoured so that, in addition to patrol duties, the tasks of the 'van Speijk' frigates can be described as:

● Long range protection of convoys and other naval groups against submarine attack.

● Short range protection of convoys and other naval groups against submarine and light surface ship attack.
● Protection of sea lanes and barriers.

Clearly, the Dutch place emphasis on the ships' ability to conduct offensive operations against submarines.

The first two ships, *Van Speijk* and *Van Galen*, were laid down in 1963 and commissioned, along with *Tjerk Hiddes* and *Van Nes* which were laid down the following year, in 1967. *Isaac Sweers* and *Evertsen* were commissioned in early 1968 and late 1967 respectively so that the RNIN received its six new frigates within the span of 15 months, after a building time of four years. The basic design followed that of the British 'Leander' but included extensive adaptation to house Dutch equipment, particularly radar, fire control, AI electronics and sonars as well as electrical generation machinery. All these items were manufactured to Dutch design in the Netherlands.

The six appeared with much the same dimensions as their British cousins and were fitted with the 4.5in Mk 6 twin turret forward, one triple-barrelled AS mortar for launching depth charges, two Seacat mountings and the Wasp helicopter. Their aerial fit drew immediate attention to the use of Dutch electronics, the Hollandse Signaalapperaten radars having been fitted: the LW02 air search and surveillance radar at the mainmast, the DA05 surface search radar and the M45 fire control director. They were given VDS as well as hull-mounted sonar. Internal compartments were similar to the British, being gas tight, and with a slight over-pressure maintained the ships are able to be fought under nuclear, chemical or biological attack. Among Dutch naval traditions is that of naming compartments after events in the career of the ship's name. One of the ratings' messes in *Isaac Sweers* is called 'Chatham'.

The original complement was designed to be 235 officers and ratings, less than the British 'Leanders', but varied during the course of operations and as minor additions were made during the first years at sea. The ships have been

Above:
The first Dutch 'Leander' — *Van Speijk* as built. Apart from the LWO2 air surveillance radar at the mainmast and DAO5 target indicator at the foremast the ship is not unlike its cousins in the RN. *RN — Osprey*

Right:
***Van Speijk* as modernised. External changes seen here include the new Oto Molara gun, Seacat and the triple torpedo tubes.** *RNIN*

Below right:
***Evertsen's* Wasp preparing to take off.** *RNIN*

employed mainly in European and Atlantic waters and have been frequent visitors to Britain.

Evertsen, for example, was deployed to the Eastern Atlantic, Mediterranean and North Sea on commissioning and took part in numerous NATO and national exercises. In the spring of 1971 it entered the Mediterranean with *Van Galen*, operated with the US Sixth Fleet and visited Odessa in the Black Sea. After a year-long refit it reported to the Flag Officer Sea Training at Portland for a two-month work-up and battle training before joining the Standing Naval Force Atlantic (STANAVFORLANT) operating in both the Eastern and Western Atlantic — and visiting a fair cross-section of ports on both sides. In 1976 the *Evertsen*, *Van Speijk* and *Zuiderkruis* joined *Ark Royal* for operations, in the Caribbean and off the east coast of the USA, which terminated in Halifax, Canada. *Evertsen* again returned to Portland for further training with the RN and rejoined STANAVFORLANT.

The pattern is similar to all 'van Speijks' for

they have been regular contributors to NATO exercises and operations and have demonstrated their professionalism in the process. They have operated in small groups and with large task groups and have won a reputation for innovation and flair as well as their ability to remain on station in the most severe weather that northern waters can present.

In the 10 years since their first commissioning they became due for modernisation, a fact recognised as early as 1969 by the Chief of the Netherlands Naval Staff. A staff was set up to determine the objectives and requirements of such a modernisation programme and a steering group was formed in 1973. They presented a plan which was approved in 1974 and shortly followed by the order of the Admiralty Council to start the modernisation of *Van Speijk* on 1 January 1977. The purpose of this modernisation was stated as being to:

● Improve the firepower of the 'van Speijk' class frigates.
● Reduce operational costs through the standardisation of guided missile equipment throughout the Navy.
● Reduce manning requirements.

The work completed to achieve this aim was extensive and spanned two years. The remaining five ships were planned to follow suit at 18 months' notice. The results were apparent externally by the replacement of the 4.5in turret with a modern 76/62 Oto-Melara automatic gun. Quadruple Harpoon launchers were fitted amidships along with two triple torpedo tubes and twin Seacat launchers. The flightdeck and hangar were lengthened to take the Lynx helicopter and the mortar battery was removed. Internally, living spaces were enlarged and the bilge system modified to dispense with the need

Right:
Isaac Sweers wears the flag of a British admiral, and is experiencing the regime of work-up under the Flag Officer Sea Training at Portland. *RN — Osprey*

Below:
Evertsen, the fifth Dutch 'Leander' to be converted, arrives at Portsmouth after post-refit trials.
Mike Lennon

to discharge oily water overboard. A garbage compactor was added to avoid the problems created by the accumulation of waste to be thrown overboard, which not only had left a telltale track but had contaminated the ocean.

So much for firepower and improved accommodation. The heart of the modernisation — and that which permitted such a dramatic increase in punch — lay in a complete revision of the sensor, weapon and command systems. This project was the result of study by a committee set up in 1967 to co-ordinate operational and technical experience in the design of weapons systems. With great importance attached to standardisation in the various classes of ship, the family of digital automatic information processing systems (DAISY) was evolved to reduce construction costs and simplify maintenance and training. As with other modern control systems, DAISY replaces a multitude of analogue calculators with a central digital computer, in this case a *signaal micromim reckoner* (SMR) with a capacity of 64,000 words. Radar, sonar and EW sensors transmit data to the computer which processes and stores the information for recall or immediate use depending upon the operator's wishes. It will construct plots, calculate courses and speeds, generate warnings, present options and control weapons systems depending upon the instructions it receives. A simple programming language in the form of standard procedures is used, thus enabling the command to react swiftly to any air, surface or submarine threat.

Van Speijk re-entered service on 5 January 1979 with a crew of 180 officers and ratings, recognisable as a 'Leander' but with a fighting capacity belonging to a new generation of ships.

Australian 'Rivers'

Although not large, the RAN is well armed and trained, technically advanced and possesses a wide range of capabilities. Indeed, the RAN, with its long standing ties with the RN, has cleverly adopted features of the USN to suit its own particular needs but, more importantly, has developed its own weapons systems and ship designs, many of which have led the world and have been adopted by other navies. Perhaps the best known of these is the Ikara AS system. At the same time the Australians have not hesitated to use Dutch radars where these were considered the more suitable. The result has been that the RAN can claim with justification that it stands among the naval front-runners in quality if not quantity.

The present fleet has capabilities in all facets of naval operations including interdiction, surface and AS warfare, naval air operations, patrol and surveillance, MCM, hydrography and oceanography and support for land operations by naval gunfire and sea transport. The role of the RAN can be briefly summarised as:

● To organise, train and equip naval forces, including naval aircraft, for war at sea.
● To provide naval support for land operations.
● To provide seaward defence of ports and anchorages.

The six 'River' class, all built in Australia, fit into this concept of a balanced Fleet and between

Below:
The general arrangement of an Australian 'River' class ship.

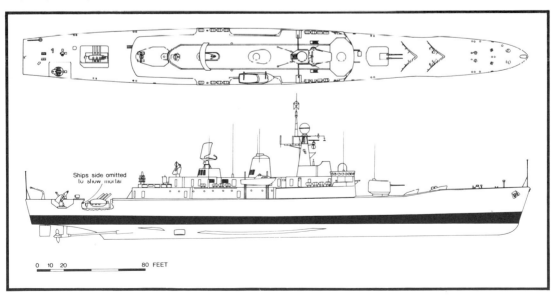

Ships side omitted to show mortar

0   10   20   80 FEET

Above:
Stuart fires the Australian AS missile Ikara. The mounting is fitted starboard side aft in Australian ships. *RAN*

the outset, an improved version of the Mk 10 (Limbo) AS mortar system, the Dutch HSA LW02 surveillance radar at the mainmast and the HSA M22 target indication and fire control radar as well as the 8GR-301 search and navigation radar. A twin 4.5in Mk 6 turret and Seacat GWS22 close range SAMs deliver the hardware. Propulsion is provided by remote-controlled boilers and geared steam turbines developing 30,000shp. Thus they are primarily AS ships although the gunnery system can be used to good effect against air and surface targets and equally well for shore bombardment. Both have a large communications complex allowing them to act as unit commanders exercising control over ships and aircraft in dispositions over thousands of square miles which modern warfare requires. Their design complement, at 250 officers and ratings, is less than the RN 'Leanders'; manning standards do not bear direct comparison but it is interesting to ponder the effect that this pressure produces in terms of design innovation.

With Ikara, the Australians felt that a helicopter was an unnecessary appendage and so flightdeck and hangar are absent. To the observer these differences will be detected in the Ikara mounting in its own well on the starboard quarter, aerial configuration, absence of clear flightdeck and, not least of all, the USN-style numbers painted at the bow. Both *Swan* and *Torrens* have seen service in Vietnam as well as conducting SAR operations in the course of their normal peacetime duties.

Swan is the 25th ship to bear the name, the first being a galley of 120 tons in Henry V's navy in 1417. The latest has achieved some distinction on the Australian station with three dramatic SAR missions. It rescued the crew of the ketch *Cutty Sark* off the East Australian coast in May 1971, and rescued an injured sailor from the MV *Austral Moon* in the steep waters of the mid-Tasman Sea. *Swan* also located and directed the rescue of the yacht *Josephine 11* stranded on the Middleton Reef in her latest lifesaving exploit. That should not suggest that the duties as a destroyer escort have been ignored because after commissioning the ship was deployed to escort *Sydney* with Australian troops embarked to the Vung Tau area during October-December 1971 and has spent long periods in South-East Asian waters both exercising and on escort duties. *Swan* has been seen in Singapore, Subic Bay, Manila, Penang, Vung Tau, Hong Kong, Kure, Takamatsu, Okinawa, has escorted the Royal Yacht *Britannia* and exercised with units of the USN, RN and RNZN. Between June 1971 and April 1972, for example, the ship steamed 47,000 miles.

Torrens has a similar record of vast distances covered and varied duties performed. The name is exclusively Australian, the first *Torrens* being one

them form the Third Australian Destroyer Squadron. The composition of this squadron illustrates perfectly the origins of their 'Leanders', for the first four — *Yarra*, *Parramatta*, *Stuart* and *Derwent* — were based on the 'Whitby' Type 12 hull with modifications to suit Australian habitability requirements and some improvements in weapons systems. The latest pair, *Swan* and *Torrens*, were based on the narrow beam 'Leander' hull incorporating increased hull scantlings and aluminium superstructure. Like the 'Leanders', the superstructure is set inboard to produce the characteristic flush upper deck. Displacing 2,700 tons, with a length of 372ft and beam of 41ft, both ships were laid down on 18 August 1965, *Swan* at Williamstown Navy Yard, Melbourne and *Torrens* at Cockatoo Island, Sydney. *Swan* was launched on 16 December 1967 and first commissioned on 20 January 1970. *Torrens* followed on 28 September 1968 and 19 January 1971 respectively. Their antecedents are clearly acknowledged in Australia by their naming and incorporation into the 'River' class, even if they have been designated with their (half) sister destroyer escorts in defiance of RN choice.

They were fitted with the Ikara system from

of six 'River' class TBDs built for the RAN between 1909 and 1916. The present *Torrens* started life with exercises off Hawaii in 1971 and since then has served as part of the ANZUK force in South-East Asia on three occasions. It too has escorted the royal yacht during the tour of Norfolk Island, the New Hebrides, Solomon Islands and Papua New Guinea during 1974. The ship has also escorted *Sydney* off South Vietnam in less joyous circumstances.

Both ships have been refitted (without major alterations) since commissioning but it is planned to modernise them in the near future. Precise plans have not been disclosed and options are clearly wide open. The principles will be to update

weapons and communications electronics, improve accommodation and reduce the crew. Whatever the future may hold for them, both *Swan* and *Torrens* have demonstrated over a decade their versatility and have responded to a

wide range of operational requirements. *Swan's* motto, 'Forward', and *Torrens'* 'Faith & Fortitude', adequately describe their reputation.

Indian 'Nilgiris'

The programme for the construction of 'Leander' class frigates in India was begun in 1964 when a collaboration agreement was concluded with Vickers and Yarrow of the UK for the construction of ships based on the broad beam 'Leander' by the Mazagon Dock Co Ltd, Bombay. It was the first construction of major warships to be undertaken by India and as the project progressed various alterations and additions were made to the original design.

Since the formation of the Indian Navy after the days of the British Raj, India has not hesitated to draw upon the experience of other maritime powers for both equipment and methods. The navy has grown under the pressure of international tension in the Middle East on one side, the Far East on the other and, not least of all, the tensions which have been manifest on the subcontinent itself. The navy, which was almost exclusively British-based in terms of both ships and tradition at the time of independence, now includes amongst its inventory a great deal of Soviet-built equipment ranging from 'Foxtrot' class submarines to 'Kashins' and 'Petyas'. Perhaps the most striking example of India's imaginative blend of foreign equipment is to be found in *Talwar* and *Trishul* — ex-'Whitby' class frigates mounting Soviet SS-N-2 missiles in triple launch tubes forward in place of the original 4.5in Mk 6 turret. There is no reason to suppose that India ignored its considerable operating experience with other ships and systems when it decided upon the 'Nilgiris' to form the Fourteenth Frigate Squadron.

The collaboration agreement provided for the transfer of design details from the MoD (UK) to the Indian Navy, the training of Indian overseers and other dockyard personnel in UK yards, the provision of UK stores items essential to the running and construction of the ships and the transfer of details of alterations and additions brought about as a result of RN experience. Finally, the agreement was extended to cover the construction of additional 'Leander' class frigates in India in the future. The construction of the first ship — *Nilgiri* — was started in mid-1966 and the programme has continued since that time. Whereas the first ship took six years to complete — as did the second, *Himgiri*, and the third, *Dunagiri*, the fourth ship of the class, *Udaygiri*, was completed within four years, being commissioned on 1 February 1977. This not only compared most favourably with other building times (UK times average at about three years) but the average cost of building the ships in India was very much less than the prices of comparable ships elsewhere. So far four have been completed; two, *Taragiri* and *Vindhyagiri* will follow in the early-1980s and, with Indian plans to form the backbone of the fleet from their frigate force, a follow-on design study is already well advanced. No doubt, as has been the case with ships already completed, each successive ship will be an improvement on its predecessor rather than a carbon copy. An order has also been placed with the Mazagon Dock Co for the construction of bigger and indigenously designed frigates incorporating lessons learned in the course of building the 'Nilgiris'.

The obvious inclusion of new ideas as the project progressed is a distinct feature of the Indian ships. The first was built entirely to the British hull design with only a lengthened hangar to take the Alouette III helicopter. It also carried the Seacat/GWS22 AA missile in one quadruple launcher, Type 965 long range air-surveillance radar, the familiar 4.5in Mk 6/MRS3 gunnery system, VDS, the Mortar Mk 10 AS close range weapons system and other British sensors. All in all, the ship looked like any other 'Leander', distinguished by the darker grey that the Indian Navy uses for its warships.

The Alouette helicopter was, however, one other obvious distinguishing feature. A direct development of the SA316B, the Indian version of the Alouette III is powered by an Astazou XIV engine providing increased efficiency and a 25% reduction in fuel consumption over the standard Turbomeca Artouste engine. The basic airframe design stretches back to 1959 and in various forms has seen considerable service around the world, becoming a well proven vehicle in the process. The 'Chetak', as the Indian version is designated, possesses a mooring harpoon for rapid securing on landing and before take-off, non-retractable tricycle landing gear with a fully castoring and lockable nosewheel and has a lift capability comparable to that of the Wasp, thus allowing the carriage of two torpedoes (or one torpedo and MAD towed astern), two AS12 wire-guided anti-ship missiles with associated gyro-stabilised sighting and Omera Orb 31 radar, depending upon the desired role. With a range of

some 375 miles and room for six passengers if cleared away it can be usefully employed for SAR duties. India has considerable experience with the military version of the Alouette III having a licence agreement for manufacture.

The second, third and fourth ships all have two quadruple Seacat launchers but with Dutch M4 directors as well as the Dutch HSA LW05 long range air-warning radar. All have sonar Type 184 but VDS is fitted only to the first three. The last pair are to be further modified to carry the Sea King AS helicopter and to this end will be equipped with Canadian Bear Trap haul-down gear, the Limbo mortar will be replaced by torpedo tubes and thus the flightdeck and hangar will be further enlarged to take the bigger aircraft.

The improvements added to later ships have gradually incorporated more and more equipment manufactured in India, culminating in the last two, *Taragiri* and *Vindhyagiri*, where all the design work created by the changes in weapons and sensors was undertaken and completed in India. They will be nonetheless clearly recognisable as of the 'Leander' family despite their very different weapons and sensor systems.

Left:
Udaygiri. The obvious concertina hangar, Seacat control radars, surface and air warning radars, and dark grey paintwork make this Indian 'Nilgiris' quite distinctive. *Mike Lennon*

Below:
Udaygiri, dressed overall, just getting underway from anchor. *Mike Lennon*

6 British Exports

New Zealand 'Provinces'

New Zealand has had a long association with the RN — since the earliest days of settlement and the acute awareness of New Zealand's dependence upon the old imperial sea routes. Fear of attack by Russian cruisers in the late 19th century prompted the government to begin regular financial contributions towards RN ships stationed in New Zealand waters which developed in to the establishment of the New Zealand Division of the RN in 1921. In 1944 this force was reconstituted as the RNZN with a built-in tradition and record of service in matters maritime. Since those days New Zealand has 'come of age' to face various problems: the USA's withdrawal from the mainland of South-East Asia; the achievement of independence by most of the island groups in the South Pacific; Britain's entry into the European Community; and the possibility of a 200-mile economic zone around its coast to police. New Zealand decided to continue the 'Core Force' concept providing a nucleus of professional forces to which additions could be made. The task of the RNZN is to provide maritime protection, with primary emphasis on escort and patrol.

To replace the ageing frigate force, *Waikato* was ordered and launched on 18 February 1965 by HRH Princess Alexandra. It was the first 'Leander' built for the RNZN and one of the first exported by Britain. A standard 'Leander', the ship was commissioned on 19 September 1966 and arrived in New Zealand in May 1967. Service in the South Pacific and South-East Asia proved so successful that a sister was ordered to be laid down on 12 April 1969 and launched as *Canterbury* by HRH Princess Anne on 6 May 1970. Basically a broad beam derivative, *Canterbury* differed from British 'Leanders' in so far as the Mortar Mk 10 was not fitted but instead two triple Mk 32 torpedo tubes were sited on 'O1' deck aft.

Waikato completed a long refit in 1977 which was, incidentally, the longest and most complex ever undertaken by the naval dockyard in Auck-

Below:
Waikato, seen in 1979. The triple Mk 32 torpedo tubes, fitted instead of the Mortar Mk 10, are to be found just abaft the sea-boat. Waikato is a narrow beam (41ft) ship. *RNZN*

land. It was extensively modernised by the installation of closed circuit TV equipment, updated communications and navigation suites and additional fuel tanks. The ship's appearance was considerably altered by extending the hangar, removing the Mortar Mk 10 and fitting TTs. The New Zealanders are now similar in looks with their extended flightdecks covering what in others is the mortar well and even the extended funnel vents which stamped *Canterbury* can now be seen on the sistership. They are fitted with British gunnery and radar systems and the Wasp helicopter.

Waikato is named after the province in North Island and the river which flows through it. Although the first ship of that name to serve in the RNZN, it was not the first to be laid down. An earlier *Waikato* was a minesweeping trawler built at Auckland and launched in 1943. Construction was suspended when the end of hostilities was clearly in sight and so it was never commissioned. The ship's badge was designed in a competition among children in the Waikato province, a Maori pupil submitting the winning entry. It depicts a tiniwha, a legendary water monster and guardian of the Waikato people and their river.

Above:
The Task Group at sea; *Waikato* takes up station
RN — Excellent

Below:
A wide beam New Zealander — *Canterbury*.
Commissioned in 1971, its hangar is enlarged to take the Lynx helicopter. *RNZN*

Above:
Dido, which has been acquired by New Zealand and is to be called Southland. *RN — Drake*

Below:
Canterbury again — but what is being carried on the flightdeck? *RNZN*

The name *Canterbury* dates from 1692 but in this case follows the tradition of naming major New Zealand warships after provinces — Canterbury being a South Island province. The ship's badge of crossed pastoral crooks over a central sheaf of wheat was designed by a student from Christchurch. The first four ships to bring settlers to the province are shown at the four compass points.

Dido has been obtained by the RNZN and renamed *Southland*.

Chile

Chile, a country of earthquakes and 4,000 miles of coastline, claims an exclusive economic zone of 200 miles and its popularity with its neighbours and the western world waxes and wanes in the variable but stiff breeze that blows through South American politics. Chile has long standing territorial disputes with Argentina in the complex chain of islands and channels which form the southern extremity of the continent and a navy which is reaching an advanced age. Modernised to some extent by the acquisition of 'Oberon' class submarines and the four 'Lurssen' class, two 'Leanders' were added to the fleet in 1975. Their progress through construction suffered the comings and goings of governments, some by fairer means than others, both in the UK

and Chile, but both units built at Yarrow's were finally delivered and steamed quietly to Chile in an effort to avoid all-round embarrassment. *Condell* (originally to have been named *Latorre* until the ex-Swedish cruiser was acquired) and *Almirante Lynch* are clearly recognisable 'Leanders' despite weapons system differences. Both have somewhat taller foremasts than others of the stable, they have no AS mortars or VDS but mount Exocet aft and retain the 4.5in gun forward. They carry Types 162, 170 and 177 sonar, 992Q surveillance radar, 965 anti-search radar, 975 navigation radar and the GWS22/MRS3 gunnery systems.

These were the last of the 'Leanders' to be built in the UK.

Above:
The Chilean *Condell*. Its flush stern — no provision at all for VDS — and aft mounted Exocet launchers are obvious but otherwise the ship looks very much like the standard 'Leander'. *Mike Lennon*

Below:
Condell from the port bow. *Mike Lennon*

7 Operations in the 1970s

It was believed that Britain's involvement in Far Eastern affairs would be virtually non-existent in the 1970s and although this did not turn out to be the absolute rule, as many 'Leanders' were to testify, the focus of RN attention had shifted towards the west. By this time the class had grown to the largest in the RN and the earlier ships had already begun a programme of modernisation. This is not to say that their employment was any less varied or at times less exciting, but with the close of the 1970s and the first 20 years in the histroy of the class it is interesting to note that not one ship had been given the ultimate test of a full scale war in which to prove itself in its primary role. The reasons for this omission may be long and complicated but include as no small ingredient the deterrent role which the ships themselves had fulfilled by their frequently demonstrated presence and readiness to act in times of crisis.

Jupiter, built by Yarrow's on Clydeside, joined the Fleet on 10 December 1969 and thus could not boast of the days off Beira or Borneo. During 1970 it operated on the West Indies station and in 1971 joined the multinational NATO force, STANAVFORLANT. The greater part of 1972 was taken up with a refit and subsequent trials programme. 1973 began with a spell on fishery protection patrol off Iceland and then a deployment to the Far East and Pacific, returning to the UK via the Americas in the spring of 1974. The ship then served for a year in Home and Mediterranean waters before entering refit at Gibraltar in October 1975. On completion of refit in July 1976 *Jupiter* emerged as the leader of the Seventh Frigate Squadron and, at the beginning of 1977, led this squadron as part of a group deployment to the West Indies and Brazil. Returning in May, *Jupiter* operated mainly in European waters including a spell as Gibraltar guardship, and attended the 60th Anniversary of the raid on Zeebrugge in April 1978 before joining a NATO exercise in the Atlantic and Mediterranean. Later that year *Jupiter* joined forces with units of the Federal German Navy for joint exercises and visited Copenhagen, Kiel, Wilhelmshaven and Hamburg before returning home to Devonport for Christmas.

Jupiter's pattern of operation during this decade illustrates a number of trends which bear closer inspection. It will be seen that the ships' refits lasted longer than those of the 1960s, a feature brought about by the increasing complexity of alterations and additions being undertaken during 'short' refits. Also, instead of ships permanently stationed in the Far East, or detached for periods of a year or so, balanced groups were deployed to distant waters for varying, but shorter, lengths of time. The period of fishery protection duties off Iceland, much publicised at the time and undertaken by many other 'Leanders', was only part of an increasing demand for protection of Britain's off-shore fishery and natural resources interests. We shall reflect more upon the Cod War but it should be remembered that these interests stretch from the North Sea and British coastal waters to the ice-edge in the Arctic. Finally, and perhaps not quite so obvious from a recital of the ship's programme, increasing integration with other NATO forces reflects not only an emphasis in defence policy but between the lines reveals the fact of Soviet expansion at sea and the eruption of her navy as an instrument of power to be wielded all over the world far beyond the requirements of defending the 'Motherland'.

Ajax, after long service with the Far East Fleet during the 1960s, entered Devonport dockyard in 1970 for conversion to an 'Ikara Leander'. On completion in 1973, it went to sea as leader of the Eighth Frigate Squadron under the command of Capt R. J. Bates RN. It undertook various tasks in 1974 ranging from guardship at Cowes to patrols off British bases in Cyprus during the troubles of that year, evacuating British nationals from Turkish-held Famagusta in August. Capt

D. J. Mackenzie led the squadron in *Ajax* on a group development which circled the world in 1975. During this deployment the ship visited Madras, Singapore, Australia, New Zealand, Fiji and Hawaii and paid the first ever official visit by a British warship to Panamanian territorial waters. The next year, 1976, Capt R. R. Squires took the ship to Canada where the town of Ajax, named after the *Ajax* of River Plate fame, granted the ship the freedom of the town. It must have been a distinct change for the ship's company to find themselves, later that same year, conducting off-shore patrol of oil and gas installations in the North Sea. Patrolling the Claymore, Piper, Beryl, Frigg, Alwyn, Ninian, Brent and Magnus fields, the ship was involved in keeping some over-zealous trawlers clear of Beryl 'A' rig. Even this was barely a warm-up, if that expression may be used, for *Ajax's* next task was of distant fishery protection on the North Cape Bank and the Skolpen Bank in the Barents Sea, boarding 19 trawlers for inspection and to give medical assistance.

Meanwhile *Andromeda*, the first of the Batch 3 Broad Beam 'Leanders', was completed in time to see service in the Far East and on the Beira patrol in 1969. In 1970/71 it was employed in home waters and on fishery protection off Iceland before deploying again to the Far East in 1972/73. Returning home in 1973 the ship was involved in further home waters exercises and Icelandic patrols. *Andromeda* too was heavily involved in the successful evacuations from Cyprus during the Turkish invasion and, in 1975, similarly active operations off Iceland. This was followed by the necessary and familiar pattern of NATO and national exercises and in the last year of its commission the ship was present at the Jubilee Fleet Review and paid a last visit to the Mediterranean (which included a spell as Gibraltar guardship) before an important diplomatic visit to Palma, Spain. Finally, *Andromeda* returned to the North Sea for offshore patrol and by the end of 1977 was again in dockyard hands, this time for major refit and conversion. *Andromeda* was, incidentally, the first ship to enter the purpose-built covered Frigate Refit Complex at Devonport. In nine years the ship had steamed 333,000 miles under the command of eight different captains.

The navigational records of other 'Leanders' show the same pattern as those of *Jupiter, Ajax* and *Andromeda*. The experience of *Diomede* gives deeper insight into the problem faced by the RN in general and 'Leanders' in particular.

Built at Scotstoun by Yarrow's, *Diomede* was commissioned on 21 May 1971 at Portsmouth and operated between Portsmouth, Portland and Chatham whilst working up. On 1 November, whilst in the Channel off Eastbourne, it was called to the assistance of the Liberian tanker, *Fspia*, of 19,959 tons, which had caught fire. Fire fighting equipment was put aboard and some of the

Espia's crew who had taken to the boats went back to fight the fire. The two crews had the fire under control in two hours. On the same day *Diomede* was allocated to the Third Frigate Squadron as Captain F3.

For the first nine months of 1972 *Diomede* made a tour of the Far East. It sailed from Portsmouth on 7 January and proceeded to Hong Kong via Gibraltar, Simonstown, Mombasa, Dubai, Bahrein, Mena al-Ahmadi, Bandar Abbas, Gan and Singapore arriving on 30 March. In May the ship

Above:
In all deployments the ship's boat is used. The coxswain of *Naiad's* boat checks the falls before lowering. Note the man ropes being held in case the boat is prematurely slipped. *MoD*

Above right:
'Awaaay Boarding Party'. The team includes a radio operator, an engineering mechanic (with tool bag and overalls), and a grapnel ready for use. The officer in charge is excused tin hat! *RN — Excellent*

visited Nagasaki and Hiroshima and on 22 May started the homeward leg visiting Subic, Singapore, Bangkok, Penang, Gan, Diego Garcia, Simonstown, Port Elizabeth, Tristan da Cunha, Montevideo, Rio de Janeiro and Las Palmas, arriving in Chatham on 29 September. Diomede spent the remainder of the year in home waters and on fishery patrol spanning Christmas and New Year. At the beginning of 1973 it went on a spring cruise to the Mediterranean calling at Gibraltar and Toulon arriving back in home waters in time to escort *Ark Royal* across the Atlantic to the West Indies. They arrived in Bermuda on 14 May and subsequently visited most of the islands in the West Indies and also Miami, San Juan, Jacksonville, Key West and Freeport. *Diomede* paid off to refit in Chatham on 5 November 1973 and relinquished command as Captain F3 to *Leander*.

During refit *Diomede* was the first RN ship to have the boiler installation converted to steam atomisation. In this system fuel and steam are injected into the furnace burners simultaneously, the steam breaking up the fuel into a fine spray to ensure complete combustion. The refit was completed on 31 May 1974, and after trials and working up the ship sailed in September to the Far East with the remainder of the Third Frigate Squadron as RN Task Group 317.2, calling at various ports round Africa before arriving in Singapore on 21 December. It left Singapore on 20 January 1975 and after exercising with units of the Thai Navy, visited Bangkok, Subic and Manila before returning to Singapore on 3 March. On 19 March the ship started its journey home calling at Gan, Mahe, Beira, Mauritius, Santos and Gibraltar, arriving in Chatham on 11 June. After the visit to Santos in May *Diomede* had exercised with units of the Brazilian Navy and was to spend the remainder of the year exercising and training round the British coast. At the end of January 1976 *Diomede* was assigned to the Icelandic patrol and remained there with only one short break until the spring. The crew had little need of an atlas of the world for the time being.

For more than six months from November 1975 news reports were full of details of the so called 'Cod War' between Iceland and the UK. Stories of rammings and warp cuttings were abundant and the dangers of close-quarters ship handling and replenishment at sea in rough weather were very much emphasised. Here, surely, was a tough test for the 'Leanders' whose sea-keeping qualities had been so often praised in the past. *Diomede* shared the doubtful pleasure of these patrols with the RFA tankers *Tidepool* and *Olwen* and the frigates *Naiad, Andromeda, Yarmouth, Falmouth, Lowestoft, Leander, Juno, Galatea, Bacchante, Scylla, Leopard, Brighton, Gurkha, Mermaid, Tartar* and *Salisbury*, all of whom had their tales of damage sustained and

damage avoided in the worst weather that these high latitudes could offer the seaman. It was shared, of course, by the trawlers themselves and all grew to admire the tenacity and skill of these deep sea fishermen which — although never doubted — had not been a familiar sight, until then, for most of the young men serving in the RN. In sustaining serious damage *Diomede's* story is of particular interest.

Diomede experienced only one gale above force 12 and only moderate icing during January but with the short days and long nights the month

Right:
View of *Diomede's* port side after collision with the Icelandic gunboat *Baldur* in April 1976. *Diomede* completed the patrol. *MoD*

Below:
Apollo as leader of 2nd Squadron. The gratings just abaft the Jackstaff are for the leadsman. *RN — Excellent*

produced the most exciting encounters with the Icelandic coastguard service, whose skill was to become the object of admiration. The first brush, with *Tyr*, developed into a chase in and out of the trawler fleet in the pitch dark at 20kt without physical contact. The second, with *Baldur*, climaxed in the ramming of *Diomede* which split the stem by bending it to port and putting a hole in the starboard bow just below the forecastle. Flooding was kept to a minimum and the ship was able to continue its patrol without any restriction.

By now the routine of the patrol had become established, with helicopters playing a major, if unusual, part. Each frigate on station had its own Wasp flight embarked, and the tankers a Wessex 3. Together these helicopters were employed on probe, plot compilation and helicopter dispatch services. Flight operations normally started before dawn, which in December and January meant some 18-20 hours each day for the flight commander to indulge in whichever pastime he might prefer when not flying. As the days passed all this changed and providing the flightdeck was in limits and icing could be

Left:
Bacchante on fishery protection duties in March 1976 off Iceland. *RN — Excellent*

Below left:
Galatea on fishery protection duties prepares to board a trawler to check its fishing gear. The photograph was taken by a Nimrod aircraft from RAF Kinloss working on area surveillance in co-operation with Galatea. *RAF*

Below:
'Leanders' in company in the Indian Ocean. The camera faithfully records the difficulties in station-keeping in line-ahead! *MoD*

Above:
Achilles **dressed overall at sea — both Jack and Ensign flying. The occasion must surely have been an exercise — note the mast-head ensign!** *RN — Osprey*

Below:
A selection in the Far East: *Naiad* **leads** *Llandaff,* *Vendetta, Dido* **and** *Yarra* **in 1971.** *MoD*

avoided, helicopters were launched to hunt for gunboats. Even so, conditions for flightdeck operations were far from ideal in the short, gloomy daylight above the arctic circle. Winds of hurricane force were experienced every three weeks or so as regular depressions swept the area and seldom dropped below 25-30kt. Surface temperature varied between −10°C and +5°C

F71

Above:
'Leanders' in the Indian Ocean — 1974. No doubt, the confusion on the port wing was resolved without rancour! *MoD*

Left:
Hong Kong. Spot *Leander* **—** *Blake* **is bottom right,** *Falmouth* **and another to the left.** *Stromness* **is the RFA.** *RAF*

and the sea state was never given the chance to settle down. Forecasting was made particularly difficult by the rapid and unpredictable movement of weather systems and it was not unusual for a ship to be sitting in a stiff breeze at +3°C whilst 50 miles away trawlers were ploughing into a severe storm force 11 at −8°C. Patchy fog did not help. Aircraft deck moves were always carried out with great caution with the flightdeck crew wearing safety harnesses to prevent their loss over the side, and in recovering aircraft it became the established practice for the officer of the watch on the bridge to warn the flight deck officer of impending 'big ones' so that landing-on could

be timed to fall between the well-known seventh waves.

The gunboats dodged among the islands close to the coast to conceal their presence from the frigates and the dawn patrol helicoter's aim was therefore to find them so that the frigates could assume a good marking position before the gunboats could get in among the trawlers. Before a close-quarters situation developed the helicopter was recovered and stowed away but the flight-deck crew remained closed up for two reasons. First, to report the position of the gunboat to the bridge when the captain was not in a position to see directly astern and, second, to act as the after upper deck emergency party in the event of a collision. At less dangerous times TV crews, newspaper reporters, stores, mail and movies were ferried around the force by helicopter since conditions almost invariably precluded boat transfers. Other comforts were obtained from friendly trawlers in the shape of baskets of fresh fish hauled from these lurching vessels at no little risk of fouling their wires and other obstructions. The flying day normally finished at dusk but when conditions allowed, night sorties were occasionally flown to identify radar contacts.

There appeared to be three distinct phases in *Diomede's* March patrol. During the first week it was involved in two collisions with *Baldur* (again) and *Tyr.* This was followed by two weeks' surveillance, the gunboats keeping a distant watch

Above:
Standing Naval Force, Atlantic. *Ariadne* in company with *Sheffield* and USS *Paul* in 1979.
RN — Flag Officer Plymouth

Above right:
Deployment to the West Indies and South America in 1977. The flotilla is in company with *Aurora, Danae, Scylla* and *Jupiter.* MoD

Right:
Apollo, Andromeda and Plymouth with Wasps hovering. Andromeda is with part of its squadron. *RN — Osprey*

on the fishing boats' activities. There were hopes that the political situation had eased but on 27 March any such optimism was shattered. *Baldur* again tried to get in amongst the trawlers whilst *Diomede* was alone, which moved in to mark the intruder. It rapidly became obvious that *Baldur's* intention was to cause major damage and a two-hour running battle ensued. During an encounter which called for 250 engine orders, *Baldur* made 30 attempts to ram by swinging her stern against *Diomede's* side. There were four collisions during that afternoon, the final one causing a 20ft hole in the wardroom at two deck level, destroying the wardroom bar in the process. Temporary repairs with shores and padding enabled *Diomede* to remain at sea without fear and the ship left the patrol as planned to make a fast passage to Rosyth.

'Leanders' had been active around the world during the decade.

8 Motive Power

'Leanders' were the last all-steam ships built for the RN and for that reason alone their machinery design is of interest. It is of even greater interest in that it represents the culmination of a tremendous co-operative design effort between the (then) Admiralty and British industry, and the RCN and Canadian industry. Its origins stem from the immediate postwar period and the object was to produce the best that could be conceived for the needs of the GP frigate.

By 1948 there was a general feeling among the Engineer-in-Chief's Department of the Admiralty that it was not going to be possible to build a modern frigate because the weight of conventional steam machinery and fuel required to give a reasonable endurance at any reasonable speed was so great that it would not fit into the size of ship normally considered as escort size. Such a ship (containing the required machinery) would be too large to be manoeuvrable and would be prohibitively expensive in terms of money, time and manpower to build. The possibility of designing a machinery system that would provide the required horsepower, endurance and efficiency at low power within the weight constraints of an escort vessel became an

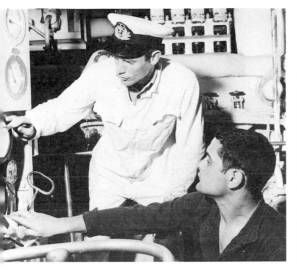

urgent design ambition. It was necessary, somehow, to reduce the total weight of contemporary machinery systems and fuel from some 45% of the ship's displacement to about 30%. This in turn meant a reduction of the order of 25% in the specific weight of machinery, in terms of lb/shp over the 'Daring' class.

Such a project was complicated by the fact that the new requirement was a reversal of the design effort then in train (essentially related to destroyers), which was looking at machinery to produce twice the power required by the new frigate design. Efforts were being concentrated on a two unit design which, although it represented an improvement, did not achieve the space and weight saving required for a frigate. The urgency of the problem was, however, great; the design team was switched to the so-called Y100 project to be led by Yarrow & Co Ltd and including members of the English Electric Co for turbine work.

The team decided to deal with the Y100 problem in a new way. Machinery design would be pursued well ahead of ship design, all ships of the class would be identical as far as the propulsion system was concerned and, finally, designs for as many individual items as possible were to be procured by competitive contract. This all seems obvious with hindsight but the principle produced complications both at the time and during later stages. It was hoped that one ship

would run well ahead of the rest of the programme so that the design could be examined, problems rectified and modifications included in the final, frozen design for the rest of the class. Furthermore, English Electric wished to compete for turbine design and therefore could not be included in the investigating team, whilst Yarrow's made it clear that it would not be submitting a boiler design.

Boiler design was competed for by four firms, the turbine by three; a vast range of auxiliary machinery designs were considered and the investigating team were satisfied that a reasonable solution to the general problem could be found. At the same time Canada was embarking on an AS escort destroyer design and decided to use Y100 machinery, order the first set in Britain, test it in Canada and thereafter set up 'line' production facilities in Canadian industry. A pressing problem became a rush to meet Canadian deadlines, the first set of machinery being required before the St Lawrence froze in 1951. The requirement was achieved and in providing the first set of machinery within $2\frac{1}{2}$ years of the start of detailed design great emphasis was placed on project co-ordination.

The Korean War placed further pressure on the organisation of a production programme and it was decided to order the first set of machinery for the Whitby class before the ships themselves had been ordered. This set another precedent, for it had always been the practice in the past for ship builders to build the turbines of the ship under construction.

Layout

In the end the requirement to reduce machinery length by 25% could not be achieved without sacrifice in damage control arrangements. Having only one engineroom and one boiler-room was accepted and another major concession given in allowing for only 50% full power to be obtained if one major component were to be put out of action either by enemy action or breakdown. Forced lubricating oil pumps were the one important exception to this rule.

Boiler design

Steam conditions which could still be regarded as conventional were decided upon so that only conventional materials need be used; 850°F at 550lb/sq in with the ability to lower temperature at lower power was selected and the final design chosen was one submitted by Babcock & Wilcox.

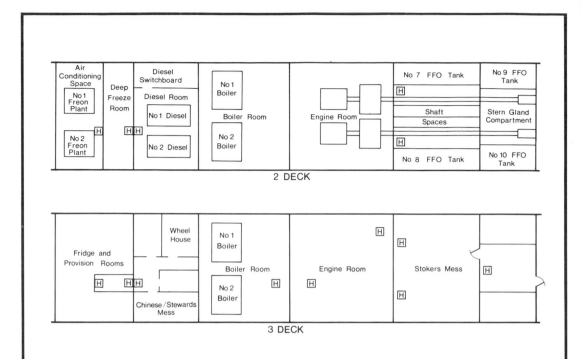

Air Conditioning Space	Deep Freeze Room	Diesel Switchboard	No 1 Boiler	Engine Room	No 7 FFO Tank	No 9 FFO Tank

Air Conditioning Space — No 1 Freon Plant, No 2 Freon Plant

Deep Freeze Room

Diesel Switchboard / Diesel Room — No 1 Diesel, No 2 Diesel

No 1 Boiler

Boiler Room — No 2 Boiler

Engine Room

No 7 FFO Tank

Shaft Spaces

No 8 FFO Tank

No 9 FFO Tank

Stern Gland Compartment

No 10 FFO Tank

2 DECK

Fridge and Provision Rooms

Wheel House

No 1 Boiler

Boiler Room — No 2 Boiler

Chinese / Stewards Mess

Engine Room

Stokers Mess

3 DECK

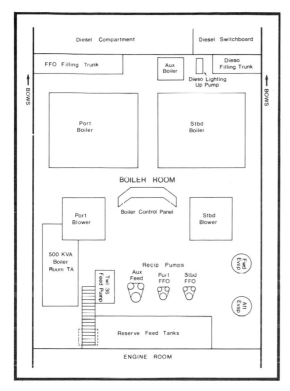

It had a low weight and a simple method of steam
temperature control by means of dampers.

Oil Burning

Y100 boiler design was based on almost exactly
double the furnace forcing rates which had been
used in the past, resulting in a very considerable
reduction in boiler size. The method of combustion adopted involved high air pressure drops
through the register, and the blowers, one per
boiler, were designed for a maximum head of
53in of water. A leakage of 3% of the full-power
air requirement through the gas casing and 3%
through the outer air casing was specified.

Turbines

The problem for turbine design was a difficult one,
for the requirement stated was for high efficiency
at very low percentages of full power and virtually
all the way up to full power. The English Electric
Co won the contract by offering a design which

included a declutching cruising turbine and one
main turbine geared to the shaft by double-
reduction locked train gearing. In this system the
cruising turbine automatically engages or dis-
engages according to its relative speed and both
turbines are controlled by a single hand-wheel
operating a set of nozzles on each turbine. The
cruising turbine can also be declutched by hand
and the main turbine alone can achieve the main
power range.

Gearing

Hobbed and shaved gears were decided upon and
a design by Messrs David Brown & Sons was
accepted for use in the RN. After extensive testing
it was found possible to reduce bearing lengths
considerably, which, particularly at low power,
would reduce bearing losses and thus an appre-
ciable proportion of mechanical losses within the
gearbox.

Water System/Pipework/Feed System

Various design innovations, in the RN ships at
least, were incorporated into auxiliary machinery
systems. Main circulating pumps, only used for
manoeuvring, were fitted outside the main
circulating system to an advanced design using a
high-speed turbine and epicyclic gearing by
Messrs W. H. Allen Sons & Co Ltd. A de-aerator
was fitted in the feed system in a shunt circuit
between the main extraction pumps and the main
feed pump. Steam system pipework did not
exceed 5in and great emphasis was placed on
reducing the size and weight of valves.

Improvements

Thus the first 'Leanders', being essentially
improved 'Whitby' type frigates, went to sea with
the Y100 propulsion systems, and benefited from
its advantages and suffered its frustrations —
cramped pipework being not the least of these.
Two improved machinery designs were to follow
— the Y136 'Leanders' and the Y160, and last,
'Leanders'.

The Y136 improvements were essentially
based upon experience gained with Y100
machinery restricted by the basic ship design
which precluded major changes to blower down-
takes ventilation trunks, uptakes and so forth. The
superheated steam system was modified to avoid
obvious stress points and valvework was reduced
by five individual valves — a saving of 18%.
Major changes were, however, incorporated in to
the boiler design by moving superheater headers
apart, giving better access to tube roots, welding
casings, arranging dampers athwartships to
eliminate backlash, and by adopting other
changes to improve accessibility. Gearing was
also changed radically by the removal of cruising

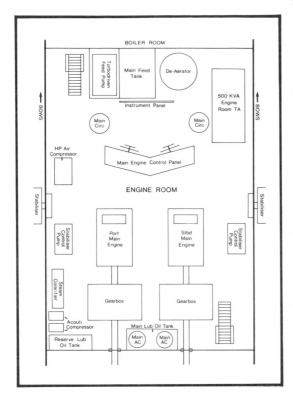

Diagram labels (Boiler Room / Engine Room layout):

BOILER ROOM

Turbo-driven Feed Pump
Main Feed Tank
De-Aerator
500 KVA Engine Room TA
Instrument Panel
BOWS
BOWS
Main Circ
Main Circ
HP Air Compressor
Main Engine Control Panel
ENGINE ROOM
Stabiliser
Stabiliser
Stabiliser Control Pump
Stabiliser Control Pump
Port Main Engine
Stbd Main Engine
Steam Collar Filter
Gearbox
Gearbox
Acousti Compressor
Main Lub Oil Tank
Reserve Lub Oil Tank
Main AC
Main AC

turbines and thus the cruising train. The broad beam 'Leanders', the last 10 of the class, were built with Y160 machinery and as such are the last true all-steam RN warships (if nuclear-powered submarines are excluded from the competition). The system is a mixture of automatic controls and remote actuators based on pneumatic systems designed and made by GEC-AEI and Telektron Ltd. Automatic controls are fitted to regulate boiler water level and auxiliary exhaust steam pressure and remote controls have been superimposed on the original Y136 machinery in the engine and boiler rooms. It is thus possible, and normal, to operate from the machinery control room. Problems with conversion to diesel fuel from the thick furnace fuel oil have been overcome by the adoption of steam atomisation which has cured boiler pulsation and flame-out in the absence of automatic control of air/fuel ratio.

One of the original objects of the Y100 machinery design was to produce a system which could be operated by wartime conscripts with comparatively little training (but, one must assume, a degree of intelligence). This led to a reduction in the number of hand controls to be operated — a single handwheel for the whole of the turbine ahead range, automatic gland steam control, automatic exhaust pressure control, closed feed system control, lubricating oil

temperature control and so on. It is strange to reflect that this concept has been expanded to encompass further automatic control in both later 'Leander' designs and the gas systems of modern ships, yet the original purpose — simplicity for conscripts — has been forgotten, if not to say abandoned. Perhaps by chance, and arguably for the wrong reasons, the original design heralded a new era in marine engineering which went beyond merely arresting a seemingly out of control power/weight/size ratio problem. Those who have kept long watches wrestling with the difficult job of controlling fans and fuel oil temperature and pressure, as well as those who have sought access to remote parts of the system to perform simple and routine maintenance may have cursed the designer with feeling. It was, however, the result of the first (and last) postwar naval steam machinery design effort and set the scene for the standardisation and remote control which is now commonplace.

9 Modernisation

It has been claimed that the 'Leanders' were the first ships to be designed with a mid-life modernisation specifically in mind. Whether this is so or not, they entered service when the advances being made in solid state electronics were obvious for all to see. The possibilities which these offered could already be seen in the space exploration programmes — and many an officer of the watch, having problems with internal communications, would complain that if it were possible to talk directly to a man on the moon, why could he not establish decipherable dialogue with the engine room? There were examples closer to home, many of which had been pioneered in Britain and already applied, piecemeal, to 'Leanders' as they went to refit. Many systems could not, however, be fitted without major alterations to existing ships and the earliest ships of the class were not yet half way through their lives. By the late 1960s every major naval power had sophisticated weapon systems at sea and their efficiency had been proven in both exercises and analytical theory. A practical demonstration had even been provided by the dramatically successful use of Styx missiles fired from patrol boats still in harbour against the Israeli destroyer *Elath* during the Egyptian/Israeli Six Day War of 1967. The 'Leanders' themselves had been used to Cold War confrontations and minor conflicts but their success in these situations provided cold comfort for their future in any major war at sea and the risk of such an event had not diminished in the slightest.

It was decided to undertake a modernisation programme to enable the 'Leanders' to continue to take their place in a modern Task Group. The original modernisation plan began in 1970, was due for completion in 1985 and divided the class into three groups or, rather, batches:

Batch 1 — The earlier eight of the class were to be fitted with Ikara in place of the 4.5in gun;
Batch 2 — The second batch of eight hulls were to have Exocet fitted in place of the 4.5in gun;
Batch 3 — The remaining ships of the class — the 10 Broad Beam 'Leanders' were to be unaltered substantially but early plans did include fitting Sea Wolf to *Andromeda*.

The best laid plans may oft go astray and Royal Navy 'Leander' modernisation has been altered somewhat to meet changed perception in requirements and, since the Falklands, to benefit from bitter experience. Sea Wolf has assumed a bigger place in the programme than originally intended and the development of sophisticated towed array sonar has also changed the scheme of things. Naturally the fit of communications, radar, sonar and EW variants to individual ships has been seemingly haphazard — the class varied as much in the build anyway with plenty of fitting 'for but not with' as systems developed.

All three batches were to have improved accommodation, renewed internal cable runs, propulsion system alterations, revised aerial arrangements, agouti, water compensated fuel systems and many other hidden alterations and additions. The 'Leander' spotter will be able to identify many subtle differences between ships.

Unmodernised Ships

Above left:
Jupiter, a pre-modernisation Batch 3 'Leander' with characteristic broad beam. A — VDS; B — Mortar Mk 10; C — Wasp helicopter; D — Single Seacat mounting; E — Seacat director; F — Type 965 long range air search radar and IFF; G — Wireless aerials (receive); H — Gun director; I — Twin 4.5in Mk 6 gun turret; J — Life rafts; K — Corvus chaff launcher; L — Hangar door; M — Landing lights. *RN — Excellent*

Below left:
Galatea (Batch 1) exposes its stem before Ikara modernisation In 1974. *RN — Excellent*

Above:
Dido (Batch 1) — a pre-Seacat 'Leander' with Bofors guns. *RN — Excellent*

Below:
Juno (Batch 2) — the class now has Seacat. *RN — Osprey*

Left:
Danae (Batch 2) in the 'races' off Portland Bill.
RN — Osprey

Below left:
A very sharp turn — almost crab motion — by Hermione (Batch 3). *RN — Excellent*

Below centre:
A clear shot of Hermione's broad stern. *RN — Osprey*

Right:
Diomede shows the flush stern of a Broad Beam 'Leander' without VDS. *RN — Excellent*

Below right:
Andromeda in the frigate refit complex at Devonport. Note that the ship is afloat in this 'drive-in garage'.
RN — Osprey

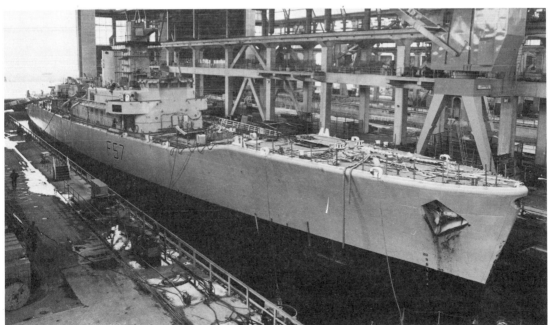

Batch 1 (Ikara) modernisation

Above:
Batch 1 (Ikara) conversion — HMS *Aurora*.
Modifications include the extra Seacat, conversion of
the 4.5in magazine to the Ikara magazine, the addition
of the two single 40/60 Bofors and, most obvious of all,
the removal of the 'key'. A — Seacat director GWS22B;
B — Seacat mountings; C — Mortar Mk 10; D — HF
aerial; E — VDS; F — IFF; G — SATCOM aerials;
H — Ikara tracker; I — Ikara mounting/launcher;
J — Single 40/60 Bofors.   *RN — Osprey*

Left:
Aurora with empty Ikara and covers shipped.
RN — Excellent

Below left:
Naiad launches an Ikara.   *RN — Excellent*

Above right:
Leander in company with *Ark Royal* and *Olmeda* off the
east coast of Scotland in 1978.   *RN — Ark Royal*

Above centre:
Ajax post-Ikara, with lowered whip aerials, 1973.
RN — Osprey

Right:
The Ikara 'vehicle' with the torpedo underneath.

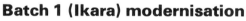

Ikara

Development of the Ikara AS weapon system was initiated by the Australian Department of Supply in the late 1950s. After extensive (and exclusive) Australian hardware development at Woomera in South Australia and at sea with the RAN it was ordered into production for the RAN in 1963. Since its concepts and development were Australian they are described in greater detail where they properly belong — under the Australian 'Rivers'. Nonetheless, the proven advantages of this extremely quick-reaction and flexible system were not lost upon other navies and represented progress which was unwise to ignore.

The RN had relied upon weapon-carrying helicopters to provide a stand-off AS system and whilst this had proved flexible and fairly quick it could hardly qualify as immediate. The logistic problems of keeping helicopters at instant readiness requires great effort and space quite impossible to achieve in a frigate. Ikara, on the other hand, is always ready in its launcher and, flying at a speed far in excess of that attained by a

helicopter, much more closely reaches the ideal of instant readiness.

Exocet GWS50

The MM38 Exocet is an anti-ship weapon developed in France at the turn of the 1960s/70s as a quick reaction defensive system. Often described as a 'hands-off' weapon, the principle of its operation is that the range and bearing of the target are transmitted to an inertial guidance system in the missile, along with a desired range which must elapse before the activation of a radar homing and flight altitude system. The missile is fired and from that moment it computes its own control orders to arrive at a predetermined position from which to begin the search and homing phase of its flight. Altitude is controlled by a radio altimeter which by its sensitivity and lookahead system allows the missile to fly some 10ft above the sea.

The manufacturers, Aerospatiale, completed their tests in 1972 and after a year of evaluation with the French and Royal (as well as German) navies it was accepted into service with some minor modifications. The missile is powered by a two-stage solid fuel rocket motor giving it a range of about 25 miles. Its cruise speed is just subsonic

Below:
Ikara in its 'pit'. *RN — Excellent*

Batch 2 (Exocet) modernisation

Above:
Batch 2 (Exocet) conversion HMS *Cleopatra*.
Modifications include Seacat update, an extended
hangar for the eventual replacement of the Wasp by
Lynx, removal of the mortar and extending the
flightdeck, fitting of torpedo tubes and conversion of
the forward magazine to Seacat for the additional
forward launcher, and various A I 0 and sonar
improvements as systems emerge. A — Helicopter
(Wasp to be replaced by Lynx); B — After Seacat
mountings; C — After Seacat director; D — Type 965
long range air search radar; E — ESM; F — Forward
Seacat director; G — Forward Seacat mounting;
H — Exocet launcher; I — Single 40/60 Bofors;
J — Torpedo tubes (STWS Mk 32); K — HF/DF.
RN — Osprey

Left:
Cleopatra bow-on. *MoD*

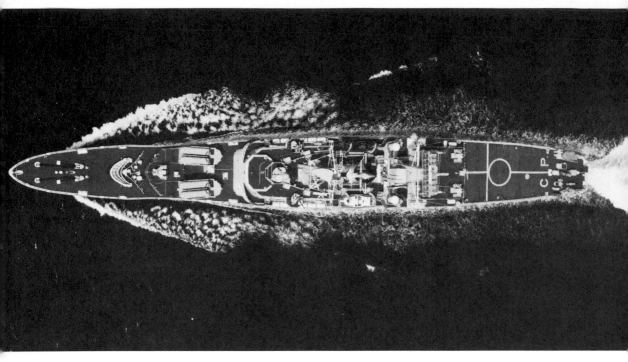

Above:
An Exocet 'Leander' from above — *Cleopatra*.
RN — Osprey

Below:
Sirius rides at anchor. *RN — Excellent*

(Mach 0.93), is stabilised by cruciform wings and controlled by tail rudders and elevators in the same plane. With a payload of high explosive its hitting power is roughly the same as the simultaneous impact of four 4.5in shells — but the probability of achieving this in a much shorter time is in the order of 90% making any further comparison a somewhat academic exercise. The missiles are stored in rectangular box containers which also serve as launchers making the problem of resupply at sea one which is yet to be completely solved.

Since its original development a longer range version, the MM40, has been developed to carry the same warhead but with an improved homing system. Its tubular glass fibre launcher-come-container may well simplify the matter of replenishment and thus provide greater flexibility in a system which was originally fitted as a highly lethal single-shot pre-emptive strike weapon for use against surface markers.

Batch 3 (Sea Wolf) modernisation

Above:
Batch 3 (Broad Beam) modernisation —
HMS *Andromeda*. Original plans called mainly for internal reorganisation — the gun mounting forward was to stay. However, Sea Wolf and Exocet have been fitted to the batch as they have become available for refitting. Various other additions appear as systems are developed. A — Sea Wolf launcher; B — Exocet launcher; C — Sea Wolf tracking radar, Type 910; D — ESM; E — Sea Wolf surveillance radar, Type 968/967; F — Pole aerial (ESM); G — Chaff launcher.
RN Osprey

Below:
Jupiter, showing the cut away port quarter to allow a clear flightdeck, after the fitting of Sea Wolf. Note the fatter foremast and the pole-type mainmast. The lines of the ship are distinctly altered from the original but with the high forecastle it could not be mistaken for any other class. *Mike Lennon*

Sea Wolf

Intentions for fitting Sea Wolf to 'Leanders' remained somewhat vague until the lessons of Exocet in the South Atlantic were painfully demonstrated. A quick reaction anti-missile missile became an urgent requirement. Of course the system was developed at sea on board *Penelope*.

To be precise, Sea Wolf/GWS25 is a point defence anti-missile system designed to give ships of frigate size and above the means of defending themselves against the close missile, air and surface threats of the 1980s. The requirement was first raised as a Naval Staff Target in 1964 and studies were begun under the codename 'Contessor'. The aim was to provide a system capable of operating under the severest environmental conditions, with a fully automatic response to threatening targets to ensure, as far as possible, that no incoming target or threat could go unengaged due to human fallibility. The system had to have a high reliability associated with automatic performance.

The requirement was to be met by a system using a command-to-line-of-sight missile, a pulse doppler radar differential tracker and a pulse doppler air surveillance radar.

The British Aircraft Corporation was nominated as missile contractors and Marconi Radar Systems as the contractor for the overall ship system with Vickers contracted for the launcher system. Firing trials took place at Aberporth, Wales and Woomera, Australia from 1970 to 1976 whilst trials of the system radars began in *Penelope* in 1975. Full missile firing trials from the ship started in 1976. The system was developed into the three major sub-systems of surveillance, tracker and launcher. Each is largely self contained and incorporates its own dedicated data processing system:

Surveillance: Two high power radars are used to detect surface and air targets. The system combines a conventional S Band radar — Type 968 — with a special self-adaptive L Band pulse doppler radar — Type 967 — the two being mounted back to back on a roll and pitch stabilised platform. Together with IFF information this data is processed by computer to form tracks, analyse threats, establish priorities and allocate targets to trackers.

Tracking: The Type 910 radar is a differential tracker using pulse doppler. By using mono-pulse an all-weather performance against small targets is achieved. After launch the missile is immediately acquired by a wide angle gathering beam and the tracker, having been guided on to the target by precise surveillance data, is able to control the out-going missile from very close in. Low level target tracking is achieved by mounting a television system on the radar tracker and aligning the camera to the radar bore sight. Target acquisition is normally carried out by radar and control passed to the television.

Launcher: The quick reaction launcher comprises six rectangular box barrels, each with its own rail system, doors and operating gear. Reloading is manual.

During development and subsequent in-service performance a high rate of success has been achieved by the system. Mean time between failure is high, mean time to repair is 10min, the system remains at 1sec notice during tests and the missile can be left in its launcher for long periods without attention. Targets against which Sea Wolf has achieved its 85% success rate include Mach 2 Petrel rockets, a 4.5in shell, and, of course, aircraft drones and targets. It was claimed at the time that the number of targets being hit by telemetry rounds was causing serious problems in target supply.

The missiles system has proved its trials reputation in service and, as well as other fleet units is fitted to *Andromeda, Hermione, Jupiter* and, eventually, other Broad Beam 'Leanders'.

Westland Lynx

The Lynx is one of three aircraft produced under the Anglo-French helicopter agreement of 1967 — the others are the Puma and Gazelle. Westland is the lead design firm for the Lynx and the HAS Mk 2 for shipborne anti-submarine and other roles is the version used in the Royal, and other, navies. The Lynx is the first British aircraft to be designed entirely to metric specification, it flew for the first time on 21 March 1971 and entered trials with Royal Navy in 1976. The unit set up for trials (700L Naval Air Squadron based at RNAS

Above:
A naval Lynx development aircraft fitted with four AS12 missiles as part of the armament trials. *Westland*

Below:
Sirius embarks a Lynx at sea. *RN — Osprey*

Yeovilton) was a joint Netherlands/British evaluation venture. Deck landing trials were completed
in HMS *Birmingham* off Portland in 1977.

The Lynx HAS Mk 2 is equipped with Ferranti
Sea Spray radar in a modified nose, and sonar
capable, the RN version of this aircraft can
conduct search and rescue, air-to-surface strike,
reconnaissance, troop transport, vertical
replenishment, naval gunfire support, communications link and, its primary role, anti-
submarine search and attack. The first production
aircraft for the RN flew on 10 February 1970 and
the first RN operational unit (No 702 Squadron —
training) was formed in 1977.

Type: Twin engined multi purpose helicopter.
Rotor System: Single four-blade semi-rigid
main rotor and four-blade tail rotor. Main rotor
blades are inter-changeable, tail rotor blades are
replaceable by opposite pairs. Main rotor blades
are manually folded and the tail rotor pylon is also
manually folded and spread.
Fuselage and Tail Unit: Conventional semi-

monocoque pod and boom structure. The forward
section has no bulkheads giving the room for
large windows and doors. Glass fibre is used
extensively in construction.
Landing Gear: Non-retractable oleo-pneumatic
tricycle. The forward twin-wheel nose unit can be
castored by the pilot and the main wheels aft are
normally locked at 27deg toe-out for deck landing
(for and aft for deck handling).
Power Plant: Two Rolls-Royce BS 360-07-26
Gem engines. Maximum continuous rating
750shp, take-off rating 830shp and a maximum
contingency rating of 900shp. Engines are
mounted side by side on top of the fuselage aft of
the main rotor and gear-box.
Armament: Combinations of Mk 44/46 ASW
torpedoes, marine markers, Mk 11 depth charges,

Sea Skua/AS12 air-to-surface missiles and machine guns.

The Lynx has proved itself versatile and handy in service. It is hardly surprising to note that 'Leander' flight commanders appreciate a twin-engined aircraft, loyal though they may be to the Wasp.

Automatic Data Handling Systems

The RN's first digital data handling system was developed in 1958 for the carrier *Eagle* and was

Below:
Weapon system profiles (*to scale*). This diagram reveals that a 'Leander' without a 4.5in gun has a restricted surface-to-surface capability — this is particularly obvious in the Batch 1 (Ikara-armed) ships. It should be remembered that the Exocet ships are limited to four missiles — any reloads must come from a supply ship. Note also that the Batch 3 ships have *either* the 4.5in gun *or* Exocet and Sea Wolf, but not both.

Right:
Before, After, and . . . *Sirius* (Batch 2) as built; post-Exocet conversion and entering the Gareloch on the River Clyde in 1978; and at anchor after fitting with the new Towed Sonar Array, the reel of which sits on an overhang to provide the extra space needed.
RN — Osprey/MoD/Mike Lennon

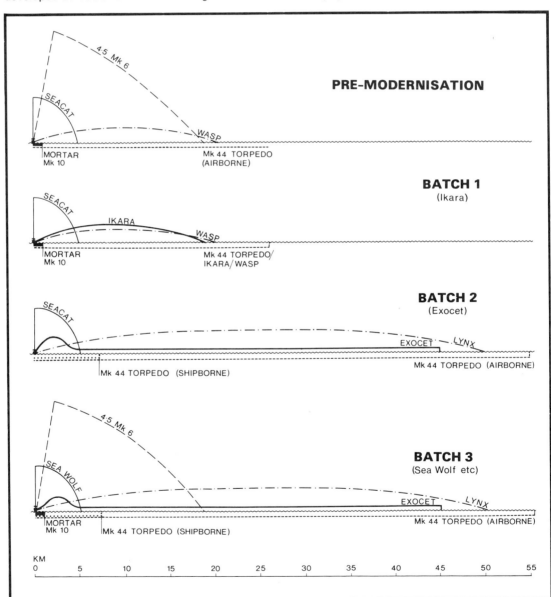

PRE-MODERNISATION

BATCH 1
(Ikara)

BATCH 2
(Exocet)

BATCH 3
(Sea Wolf etc)

Above and below:
Before and After. *Andromeda*, a Broad Beam (Batch 3) 'Leander', as Captain (F), and post Sea Wolf Conversion in January 1983. *RN — Excellent/Mike Lennon*

conceived as an air defence system based on the general purpose Ferranti Poseidon digital computer. The result was Action Data Automation (ADA), which was followed closely by an improved design for the 'County' class guided missile destroyers providing both missile direction facilities and surface and subsurface data. Detailed operational functions remained in the hands of analogue computers in these early systems and it was not until the mid-1960s that development work on the present generation of command & control systems began in earnest. The Ferranti 1600 computer provided the capacity to combine all the ship's weapons and sensors into a single comprehensive system and the action data automation weapon system (ADAWS) series was produced. Whilst ADAWS was intended primarily for large ships the need to equip frigates with a digital system was recognised and fulfilled by the computer assisted action information system (CAAIS) using the Ferranti FM1600B computer performing similar action information tasks to ADAWS including weapon direction and target indication but not fire control.

The Ferranti FM1600 and FM1600B processors are both fast, micro-programme computers, the main difference between the two being that the basic clock speed is 2.25MHz in the FM1600 and 3.0MHz for the FM1600B. Both employ a 24-bit data word and operate in the parallel mode. The address code used enables a single instruction word to specify the function to be carried out, the location of the two operands required to perform the function and the location of the result of performing that function. By using a simple programme language it is possible to use the full store capacity of the machines.

These data handling systems have not only improved reaction times of existing weapons systems but were a basic prerequisite for fitting additional and more sophisticated weaponry.

10 Some Unusual Assignments

No exercise, cruise or operation is ever the same. Ships are sent to sea or diverted at short notice to react to rescue missions, surveillance operations, civil distress ashore and a host of other possibilities. Ships are called upon to provide facilities for high level political meetings, receptions for independence celebrations and they provide guards for memorial services, working parties for building playgrounds and reparing broken down yachts (and even larger vessels), and fight fires ashore and at sea — every ship has its own tale to tell. During the winter of 1978/79 *Scylla* played host ship to two receptions given by Mr Callaghan, the first at Guadaloupe when President Carter was guest of honour, the second in Barbados, to be followed by being present in support of Princess Alexandra at the St Lucian independence celebrations.

It is not easy to define precisely what is unusual or usual but three tasks undertaken by 'Leanders' must surely fall into the category of the former.

Penelope — Trials Ship

After a first commission, *Penelope*, which had anyway been laid down as *Coventry* but launched as a 'Leander', was refitted and recommissioned as the trials ship for the Admiralty Underwater Weapons Establishment. The 4.5in turret had been removed and the hangar converted to laboratories and workshops. A Devonport ship, *Penelope* was destined to spend most of its working days running from Portland (or Gibraltar, when winter conditions in the English Channel proved too unwelcoming) conducting a series of experiments. The ship was not the first by any means to have been used in this way and not

Above right:
Dressed overall and firing a gun salute. *Scylla* demonstrates the ship's proficiency at Portland for the work-up staff. *RN — Excellent*

Right:
***Penelope* with twin 4.5in gun removed, a condition which marked the ship for many years.** *RN — Osprey*

even the first to be specifically devoted to trials. *Verulam* and the old 'Hunt' class destroyer *Brocklesby* had done similar work and *Girdle Ness* had been extensively altered to accommodate the development and proving at sea of Seaslug. *Penelope* was, in the fullness of time, able to claim that it had replaced all of them. The ship had an advantage over them in that any results achieved could be applied directly to the ships for which the particular trial in question was being conducted.

The first trials were concerned mainly with developing hull-mounted sonars and mostly con-ducted off Portland. The Type 184 scanning sonar, to become a standard fit in the class, was developed almost exclusively in *Penelope* after many long hours pinging at 'clockwork mouse' submarines. Another project, less exciting at first glance, was to occupy the ship's time for several years and was eventually to place it in some very unusual situations.

Penelope became the platform for a major investigation into propeller design and self and radiated noise. Quite apart from being wired for sound — literally — viewing ports were cut so that the propellers could be scrutinised from close range. The ship was also fitted with a variety of portable generators, normally sited on the flight-deck, so that the ship's machinery could be shut down at the behest of the scientists without depriving them of electrical power for their instru-ments. The ship's company became experts on the art of cold buffet lunches and finding their way in the gloom but the climax to this trial came in 1970 off Gibraltar when *Penelope* became a world record holder by being towed as a 'dead' ship by *Scylla* at 23kt. The tow required a specially manufactured braided nylon rope 11in in circumference and one mile in length. Some neat seamanship avoided the more catastrophic effects of the stretch which this line held in latent reserve but the data gathered has been incor-porated to feature in the remainder of the class as well as other, newer classes. If the subtleties of this contribution to modern warship design have been hidden in a welter of more dramatic developments, their effect has been of funda-mental significance in many aspects of under-water warfare. One aspect, not called for by the trial, will be remembered by the engineers of

Scylla for they discovered the effect of prolonged periods at maximum power on their propulsion system, not least of which was the exposure of each and every imperfectly finished joint in the steam range.

After its 1972 refit *Penelope* was again modified, this time to become the trials ship for the GWS25 Sea Wolf missile system. This system is designed to counter small, fast missile targets, although its application in other ways is obvious. It consists of surveillance and tracking radars with bore-sighted TV cameras on a stabilised mounting (in *Penelope's* case on the aft superstructure) and a six-barrelled launcher on the 'flight' deck. One radar detects low level targets and the other looks for high level contacts up to 75 degrees elevation. Tracking and guidance is achieved by using pulse-doppler techniques measuring small angular distances without moving the mounting. Once the in-flight missile is acquired the tracker radar switches to narrow beam so that it can track close to the sea surface. *Penelope* completed these trials in 1977 and was accepted into refit in 1978 for conversion to batch IIB, retaining the Y100 machinery. Meanwhile Sea Wolf will be fitted to Type 22 destroyers and, in the first instance, in *Andromeda*.

Television Star

In 1973 *Phoebe* underwent a conversion which became familiar to millions through the medium of television. The work involved was minimal as far as reconstruction was concerned for it was virtually restricted to changing the ship's nameboards to read *Hero*. It was relieved of this duty from time to time by other ships but, in each case, they had more work to do for *Phoebe's* pennant number, F42, was used throughout. *Hero* sailed from adventure to adventure across the cathode ray tube in a series which portrayed life in a 'Leander' class frigate with remarkable accuracy and realism. The production of this series involved the ships concerned and their sailors with both amusing and embarrassing moments. It was not long before the actors had become extremely adapted to the roles they played and were frequently taken as ship's officers or ratings by those newly joined and unfamiliar with the real ship's staff. On most occasions this confusion amounted to little more than the odd case of mistaken identity but at least once precipitated a near sense-of-humour failure. The ship concerned, alongside in one of the Royal yards, had been rehearsing all morning for the 'Admiral's' inspection of *Hero*. 'Senior officers' had been coming and going with monotonous regularity to receive the proper marks of respect at the gangway with no confusion at all. Meanwhile, out of shot, members of the ship's company had been employed painting the ship's side and they, as sometimes happens on fine sunny days at these times, were enjoying the fresh air and the opportunity to talk casually among themselves, relaxed in the knowledge that the ceremonial at the flightdeck was not their concern. As also tends to happen on these (and any other) days the captain of the dockyard chose to walk his parish and ensure all was well. On approaching *Hero*, he received no obvious mark of recognition from the painters and upon enquiring why this should be so, being unknown to them, was informed precisely, and in vulgar terms, what he and his actor friends could do with their television cameras.

There is no precise way of measuring the effects of this popular television series but it was certainly enjoyed by the 'Leanders' and whether the audience were inclined to believe it or not, formed an excellent record of life in a British frigate.

Work Study

A far less popular event in the lives of every 'Leander' ship's company in the 1960s and 70s

Phoebe? It is in fact *Dido*, disguised as *Hero* (of TV Fame), in the Medway in 1975, and still a Bofors 'Leander' at the time. *MoD*

Above:
**The real *Phoebe* with not a soul in sight before
conversion in 1977.** *RN — Excellent*

Below:
**Preparing the tow messenger. All aspects of naval work
are subject to the scrutiny of the work study teams.**
RN — Excellent

was the arrival of the work study team. The RN
was quick to recognise the potential of work and
management studies and, indeed, pioneered
many techniques which are used in industry as
standard method. In a sense a warship is ideal for
such investigation for not only is it a complex
collection of different and interdependent processes, but there has always lingered the suspi-
cion that these were conducted in accordance
with outworn tradition resulting in a great waste
of manpower and effort. Furthermore the
introduction of new technology into the Fleet
deserved the closest scrutiny to ensure that the
maximum advantage of these innovations could
be realised.

With 26 ships of the class projected and then
achieved, the 'Leanders' were obvious ground for

study. The results could be applied to a large
section of the RN in the circumstances under
which they had been arrived at in an individual
ship, and they could be analysed under various
conditions in different ships with their own views.
This feedback was to prove particularly important
in eradicating the impersonal generalisations
which can so often creep into this type of study.

A wide range of studies were undertaken and
are still in progress. Evolutions such as replenishment at sea, the Watch and Quarter Bill, maintenance routines, internal communications, exercise
routines, drafting cycles and cleaning stations
among many others received close attention. In
most cases areas for considerable improvement
were identified and procedures amended accord-
ingly. Change was not the inevitable result of
these studies, the traditional divisional system
being one prime example.

A ship's company is, and has always been,
divided into divisions according to department —
seaman, weapons, propulsion, etc — and further
into sections of employment. The precise designation varies between types of ship but the
principle is universal. Each division is led by an
officer with senior ratings under him and they are
made responsible for the welfare and advance-
ment of each member of that division. Management studies recommended various procedures
to ensure that the rigours of a modern ship did not
interfere with the workings of this system and
that its structure remained intact. On the other
hand studies recommended some changes in job
description and responsibilities which have been
adopted throughout the RN but, again, without
undermining the principle of personal
responsibility which is essential to the efficient
running of a ship.

These studies, which have changed the shape
of the RN to cope with modern equipment and
methods, were conducted largely in ships of the
'Leander' class.

11 Operations in the 1980s

The 1980s have already seen a period of great heartsearching for the RN. There has been great pressure placed upon the frigate and its ability to contribute has been seriously questioned. Meanwhile, those serving in 'Leanders' at sea seemed to have little time to ponder the finer points of landsmen's views of their place in maritime power — those in dockyard hands were equally engaged in the timeless struggle to get out of the yard.

The campaign to recapture the Falklands came as a salutary reminder, deserves its own account and, some have argued, is not typical of the task that will have to be faced at sea. The 'Leanders' that earned the latest battle honour in the South Atlantic had not been idle before they were called upon to join that famous Task Force and have been given little respite since.

There are still the Group deployments to the Far East and Australasia. 'Leanders' are seeing service in familiar haunts around Indonesia and meeting their half sisters of Australia and New Zealand. At the same time there remains the onerous and very demanding task of maintaining a presence in the Indian Ocean and Gulf Areas and this has much of the flavour of the old patrols off Beira and the very same Gulf. Now Aden is a Soviet base. Iran and Iraq are engaged in a running squabble whilst the world watches anxiously. The main feature of life for the frigates sent to patrol the area is one of slightly edgy routine with long periods at sea simply waiting.

The 'Leanders' which spent so much time east of Suez during earlier decades would find the circumstances familiar.

The demands of the North Atlantic Alliance have not ceased in the meantime. Indeed the new towed array 'Leanders' have a special place in the AS task in waters where earlier the same ships found themselves fending off Icelandic gunboats. The weather has not changed and sea-keeping is as important in this game of high technology stealth as it ever was. STANAVFORLANT continues to operate on both sides of the Atlantic and Dutch and British 'Leanders' continue to cruise in company in this group as they do in every other exercise.

Some of the 'Leanders' are now elderly ships in their 20s. Much has changed in design concepts in their lifetime and not all of that change has been for the worst. Yet the modernised 'Leander' is still a powerful ship even though some would say that its fine lines have been ruined. They continue to serve in every ocean of the world. New Zealand has acquired another 'Leander', *Southland* (ex-*Dido*) and the Indian construction programme continues. The class has not yet seen the end of its long commission.

Below:
The 1980s will see many changes of equipment for much of the class, including the new Lynx helicopter. Since the photograph *Sirius* has also been equipped with the new towed array sonar. *RN — Osprey*

The South Atlantic — 1982

Much has already been said, written and argued about British operations in the South Atlantic during the southern autumn and winter of 1982. No doubt yet more will be said before this remarkable campaign is finally considered to have been laid to rest as ancient history. In all the glare of publicity at the time *Andromeda*, *Argonaut*, *Minerva* and *Penelope* (and their cousins *Plymouth* and *Yarmouth*) served as valiantly as any; they deservedly received the battle honour 'Falkland Islands 1982' on 25 October 1983.

The big ships naturally caught the attention of newsmen and so did the gallantry of those ships lost. So it should be, but it is also worth remembering that throughout these events 'Leanders' served as close escorts for the landings, on the gun line, in the open ocean and often on their own in support of resupply shipping — indeed, at a time when it was possible to argue that the frigate's place with a Task Force at sea was a relic of the past, 'Leanders' were not absent from their place of duty. Their performance during those days far from any form of shore support is worthy of closer scrutiny.

On 2 April 1982 Argentine forces invaded the Falklands Islands and the next day, South Georgia. Two days later, on 5 April, *Hermes* and *Invincible* left the UK to catch up units already on their way, but having the dubious advantage of starting a little closer to their destination by being deployed straight from Gibraltar just before coming home from a routine deployment. Eventually over 110 ships were deployed — 44 warships, 22 from RFA and 45 merchant ships. The object of their attention lay 8,000 miles from the UK and over 3,500 miles from the nearest possible forward operating base (Ascension Island) yet only 400 miles from Argentina. This was a Task Force of a size and composition not envisaged even when the 'Leanders' first went to sea nearly 20 years earlier. They now became part of a force which within seven weeks assembled 28,000 men, sailed to the other end of the world, effectively neutralised the Argentine navy, fought off air attacks and finally put ashore 10,000 men, who marched across some of the most unpleasant ground in the world to seal the success of the operation.

Argonaut was assigned to the amphibious group on arrival in the battle zone. By the time D-Day arrived the ship had stripped itself for action, the reality of the loss of the *Sheffield* had struck home and any earlier thoughts that somehow the crisis would disappear or that the whole thing would be a walkover had long since given way to grim determination. *Argonaut* quietly slipped into the glassy calm waters of the Falkland Sound before dawn on 21 May as the larger amphibious ships pressed on to the San Carlos anchorage. The escorts went to their protective stations to await dawn and the inevitable air attacks. They were not to be disappointed.

During the 10 hours of daylight some 15 air attacks were directed at the *Argonaut*, the crew being bombarded by an assortment of Aeromacchi, Skyhawk and Mirage aircraft. They spent all day at action stations grabbing what rest and refreshment they could between attacks and seeming to invite yet another bombing run every time they paused for coffee. The amphibians were able to unload without casualty, if not exactly out of danger, and the final result of this auspicious

start to land operations is well enough known. *Argonaut* was to remain in the amphibious operating area for the next nine days conducting a harrowing battle of its own.

Towards the evening of that first day inshore the ship attracted the attention of six Skyhawks and, although one was successfully shot down and others discouraged thereby, *Argonaut* was struck. Whilst steaming full ahead towards the shore in an evasive manoeuvre bombs jammed the rudders and both engines in that configuration. The ship was saved from going aground by the quick letting go of an anchor to stop the ship, an action which required not only quick thinking and athletic achievement in getting to the forecastle but considerable courage and coolness in an exposed position. Two 1,000lb iron bombs delivered that day lodged in the ship but failed to explode — one in the boilerroom and the other between two missiles in the forward magazine. The task of clearing these hazards and restoring movement to the ship now began.

The bomb in the flooded magazine proved too dangerous to defuse in situ and it was decided to remove it from the magazine and hoist it overboard — a matter of clearing ammunition and cutting through bulkheads to gain access. Any jolt was liable to detonate the offending bomb as would any disturbance of the precise lifting angle

during its removal. The chances of the ship surviving an explosion in its magazine were remote. For the next nine days Fleet clearance divers and the ship's company worked steadily at their dangerous tasks. They came under attack themselves as the battle raged on around them. They saw the tragic losses of *Antelope* and *Ardent* and all the time they brought *Argonaut's* weapons to bear to contribute to the defence of the landing force. *Argonaut* survived, left San Carlos under its own steam and made the passage home through the winter storms of the South Atlantic as well as the balmier waters of the tropics.

Argonaut's commanding officer, Capt C. H. Layman MVO, RN, was appointed a Companion of the Distinguished Service Order for 'his calm and determined approach in this most unnerving of situations, which would have broken many . . .' Lt-Cdr B. F. Dutton QGM, RN, was similarly honoured for 'his staunch determination, steadfastness and courage of the highest order' whilst in charge of the Fleet clearance diving team removing the bomb from the magazine. Sub-Lt P. T. Morgan RN saved the ship from certain wreck by racing to the forecastle with two others and letting go the anchor. He was awarded the DSC for his 'qualities of cool and quick thinking, as well as courage and stamina, in carrying out all his duties'. Able Seaman Ian Boldy, 20, and Seaman Mathew Stuart, 18, of the *Argonaut* gave their lives in the action. San Carlos Water was to become known as Bomb Alley.

Briefly told, *Argonaut's* story is a tribute to the ship's company and to *Andromeda*, *Minerva* and *Penelope* as well as the entire class. The Falklands campaign was the RN's first experience of battle in the missile age; it was in many ways unique, but in testing resolve, the flexible use of forces, equipment and tactics it provided no less a measure of the 'Leander' class's performance. The ships were never intended under these circumstances to be other than an integral part of the overall force and so it is to overall results and

shortcomings one should look in order to judge success.

The campaign at sea was fought on the traditional principles of containing the enemy, maintaining defence in depth and keeping the initiative. Within range of enemy aircraft, in the face of a submarine threat but without the help of early warning of air attack or land-based fighters, the Task Force sustained losses — a total of four warships, one auxiliary and one merchant ship lost in addition to eight warships and two auxiliaries which were damaged in varying degrees — but clearly demonstrated the wisdom of the balanced fleet. In most cases of damage ships made good repairs and continued to take their full part in operations. The 'Leanders' suffered none of the problems faced by more modern ships in structural terms and their equipment coped well with the challenge of sometimes unfamiliar tasks and the long sea passage before the battle. The operational availability of their equipment was more than adequate to the task.

The force relied on a mix of systems for air defence including electronic detection systems, carrier-borne fighters (Harriers), ECM, missiles, medium guns and finally, point defence systems. In all they accounted for at least 72 enemy aircraft and probably 14 more. The figures provided tell part of the story but perhaps not all. The Sea Wolf system, after those years of trial in *Penelope*, whilst claiming five Argentine aircraft attacking at low level, was not fully tested against sea-skimming missiles. Nonetheless, its flexibility, speed of reaction and, above all, battle-readiness were proven beyond doubt.

Weapon System Results against Aircraft

System	Confirmed	Probable
Sea Harrier (with missiles)	16	1
Sea Harrier (cannon)	4	2
Sea Wolf	5	—
Sea Dart	8	—
Seacat	8	2
Rapier	14	6
Blowpipe	9	2
Stinger	1	—
Guns	7	1
Total	72	14

There was a constant submarine threat to ships at sea thus placing a very dangerous risk in the way of the 9,000 personnel, 100,000 tons of freight and 95 aircraft carried by merchant ships alone (the supply chain carried 400,000 tons of fuel and carried out some 1,200 transfers of ammunition, fuel and dry stores as well as 300 helicopter transfers to ships at sea). No Argentine submarine successfully attacked the Task Force. ASW lends itself to even more complicated analysis than air warfare for the very threat ties down great effort. By any measure the ASW campaign in the South Atlantic was a success for the British Task Force.

It is fitting that 'Leanders' should have joined an operation similar to those envisaged at the time of their design and in so doing to have acquitted themselves so well. That they did so is testament to their builders, designers and crews. This success was not built either in the South Atlantic or during the hurried preparations on the passage south. Generations of seamen before the present crews laid the foundations of achievement. The ships finally had the chance to prove that they were adequate to the tasks set them in the face of determined opposition as well as their general duties carried out with equal efficiency in the Far East and North Atlantic during earlier crises. Another battle honour was won by a small proportion of the class but it belongs in large part to every 'Leander' and its ship's company, past and present.

Below:
A 'Leander' steams into an impending storm off Cape Wrath. Who really knows what the future holds in store for the 'Leanders'? *MoD*

Appendices

1 Names, Honours and Associations

ROYAL NAVY

Achilles
Name: The chief hero of Homer's Iliad, son of Peleus and Thetis
History: The name dates from 1744
2. 60-gun ship of 1757
4. 3rd rate. Prize taken in 1794
5. 3rd rate of 1798
6. Armoured ship of 1863
7. Cruiser of 1905
8. Cruiser of 1932. Sold to India in 1948
Honours: Belleisle 1761; Trafalgar 1805; Walcheron 1809; River Plate 1939; Guadalcanal 1942-43; Okinawa 1945
Associations: The Borough of Afan, South Wales; the Achilles Association, New Zealand; Kent Evening Post, Chatham; Medway Society for Mentally Handicapped Children; Department of Social Services, Harrow, TS *Echo*, Llanelli; CCF Maidstone grammar school; 1st Hampton Hill sea scout group 'Achilles'

Ajax
Name: There were two Greek heroes named Ajax who played prominent parts in the Trojan war
History:
1. 3rd rate of 1767
2. 3rd rate of 1798
3. 3rd rate of 1809
4. Ex-*Vanguard*, renamed in 1867
5. Turret ship of 1880
6. Battleship of 1912
7. Cruiser of 1934
Honours: St Vincent 1780; Off Martinique 1780; Chesapeake 1781 and 82; St Kitts 1782; The Saintes 1782; Egypt 1801; Calder's Action 1805; Trafalgar 1805; San Sebastian 1813; Baltic 1854-55; Jutland 1916; River Plate 1939; Mediterranean 1940-41; Matapan 1941; Greece 1941; Crete 1941; Malta Convoys 1941; Aegean 1944; Normandy 1944; South France 1944
Associations: Truro, Cornwall; Ajax, Ontario, Canada; TS *Pellew*, Truro (sea cadets); TS *Ajax*, Swansea (sea cadets); Maidstone grammar school CCF; St Christopher's Hostel for Mentally

Handicapped Children, Redruth, Cornwall; Lancaster Court Children's home, Manchester

Andromeda
Name: Daughter of Cepheus, King of Ethiopia, who chained her to a rock as a sacrifice to a sea monster, a fate from which she was saved by Perseus
History:
1. 5th rate of 1777. Lost in a hurricane in 1780
2. 5th rate of 1784
3. Prize (*Hannibal*) taken in 1812
4. 5th rate of 1829
5. Cruiser of 1897. Later renamed *Powerful II*
Two small vessels since
Honours: Ushant 1778; Off Martinique 1780; St Vincent 1780; Falklands Islands 1982
Associations: Bull Point primary school, Plymouth

Apollo
Name: The sun god
History:
1. ex-*Apollon*, prize taken in 1747. Wrecked in 1749
2. ex-*Glory*, renamed 1744
3. 5th rate of 1794. Wrecked in 1799
4. 5th rate of 1799. Wrecked in 1804
5. 5th rate of 1805
6. Cruiser of 1891
7. Cruiser of 1934. Transferred to the RAN in 1938
8. Minelayer of 1943
Honours: St Vincent 1780; China 1842; Black Sea 1854; Normandy 1944
Associations: TS *Apollo*, Marlow (sea cadets); TS *Undaunted*, Jersey (sea cadets); TS *Scarborough*, Scarborough (sea cadets); 1st Bn, the Green Howards; Frederick Bird junior school, Coventry; Hakin CP mixed junior school, Milford Haven; Society of Friends of Scarborough ATC and Hostel of the Handicapped; children's ward of St Mary's hospital, Portsmouth; Sunnyside children's home, Scarborough; 11th Havant (Apollo pack) sea scouts/cubs

Arethusa

Name: Name of one of the Nereides who was changed by Artemis into a fountain
History:
1. Prize (*Arethuse*) taken in 1759. Lost in 1779
2. 5th rate of 1781 ('The Saucy Arethusa')
3. 5th rate of 1817. Renamed *Bacchus* in 1844
4. 4th rate of 1849
5. Cruiser of 1882
6. Cruiser of 1913. Mined in 1916
7. Cruiser of 1934

Honours: Ushant 1778 and 1781; St Lucia 1796; Curacoa 1807; Black Sea 1854; China 1900; Heligoland 1914; Dogger Bank 1915; Norway 1940-41; Malta Convoys 1941-42; Normandy 1944

Argonaut

Name: A member of the crew of the ship *Argo*, in which Jason sailed in quest of the Golden Fleece
History:
1. 3rd rate. Prize (*Jason*) taken in 1782
2. Cruiser of 1898
3. Cruiser of 1941

Honours: Arctic 1942; North Africa 1942; Mediterranean 1942; Normandy 1944; South France 1944; Aegean 1944; Okinawa 1945; Falkland Islands 1982

Associations: Manor House school, Honiton; TS *Malaya*, Derby (sea cadets)

Ariadne

Name: Daughter of Minos, King of Crete, and wife of Dionysus (Bacchus)
History:
1. 6th rate of 1776
5. 6th rate of 1816
6. Frigate of 1859. Renamed *Actaeon* in 1905
7. Cruiser of 1898. Torpedoed in 1917
9. Minelayer of 1941

Honours: St Lucia 1778; Grenada 1779; Ostend 1798; New Orleans 1814

Associations: The town of Scunthorpe; TS *Ariadne*, Scunthorpe (sea cadets); TS *Portcullis*, Wallingford (sea cadets); Clarendon School for the mentally handicapped

Aurora

Name: The goddess of dawn
History:
1. Prize (*Abenaise*) taken in 1758
2. 5th rate of 1766. Lost at sea in 1769
3. 6th rate of 1777
4. 5th rate. Prize (*Aurore*) taken in 1793
5. 5th rate. Prize (*Clorinde*) taken in 1814
6. Frigate of 1861
7. Cruiser of 1887

8. Cruiser of 1913. Transferred to the RCN in 1920
10. Cruiser of 1936. Sold to China in 1948

Honours: St Lucia 1778; Minorca 1798; Guadeloupe 1810; China 1900; Dogger Bank 1915; Norway 1940; *Biscmarck* Action 1941; Malta Convoys 1941; Mediterranean 1941-43; North Africa 1942-43; Sicily 1943; Salerno 1943; Aegean 1943-44; South France 1944

Associations: The City of Bradford (started in warship week 1942); Myrtle Park first school, Bingley, Bradford; Charlestown county primary school, St Austell; TS *Aurora*, Bradford (sea cadets); TS *Wakefield*, Wakefield (sea cadets); MV *Sparkle* — motor vessel of the Society of Sportsmen Pledged to Aid Research into Crippling (SPARKS); The Aurora works, RA Lister Co Ltd, Dursley, Gloucs

Bacchante

Name: A female devotee of Bacchus, god of wine
History:
1. 6th rate. Prize taken in 1803
2. 5th rate of 1811
3. Frigate of 1859
4. Corvette of 1876
5. Cruiser of 1901
6. Name of naval base at Aberdeen, 1939-45

Honours: Cattaro 1814; Burma 1885-86; Heligoland 1914; Dardanelles 1915-16

Charybdis

Name: A monster inhabiting a whirlpool in the Strait of Messina
History: The name dates from 1809
3. Corvette of 1859
4. Cruiser of 1893
5. Cruiser of 1940. Sunk by E-boats in 1943

Honours: Malta Convoys 1942; North Africa 1942; Salerno 1943; Atlantic 1943; English Channel 1943; Biscay 1943

Associations: The island of Guernsey; The Charybdis Association; Mayflower Darts Association Help the Children Fund

Cleopatra

Name: Daughter of Ptolemy Auletes, King of Egypt, and lover of Anthony (69-30BC)
History:
1. 5th rate of 1779
2. 6th rate of 1835
4. Corvette of 1878
5. Cruiser of 1915
7. Cruiser of 1940

Honours: Dogger Bank 1781; Martinique 1809; Burma 1853; Belgian Coast 1916; Malta Convoys 1942; Sirte 1942; Sicily 1943

Danae

Name: Daughter of Acrisius, King of Argos, and mother of Perseus (who was later accidently killed by his grandfather)

History:
1. 5th rate. Prize taken in 1759
2. 5th rate. Prize taken in 1798
3. 5th rate. Prize (*Vaillante*) taken in 1798. Carried by mutineers into Brest in 1800
4. Corvette of 1867
5. Cruiser of 1918

Honours: Normandy 1944 (in Polish service)

Associations: TS *Danae*, Chesterfield (sea cadets); Chesterfield & District Association for Spina Bifida and Hydrocephalus; Chesterfield & District Association for Mentally Handicapped Children

Dido

Name: A Tyrian princess who founded Carthage and committed suicide on a funeral pyre for grief at the departure of her lover, Aeneas

History:
1. 6th rate of 1784
2. 5th rate. Prize (*Didon*) taken in 1806
3. Corvette of 1836
4. Corvette of 1869
5. Cruiser of 1896
6. Cruiser of 1939

Honours: Toulon 1793; Egypt 1801; Syria 1840; China 1842; Zulu War 1881; China 1900; Crete 1941; Sirte 1942; Mediterranean 1942-44; Malta Convoys 1942; Sicily 1943; Salerno 1943; Aegean 1943; Anzion 1944; South France 1944; Arctic 1944

Associations: The Borough of Bolton (started in warship week 1941); various Bolton charities

Diomede

Name: Properly Diomedes, King of Argos, who went to Troy with 80 ships and was, next to Achilles, the bravest hero in the Greek army

History:
1. 4th rate of 1781. Wrecked in 1795
2. 4th rate of 1798
3. Cruiser of 1919

Honours: Cape of Good Hope 1806

Euryalus

Name: Companion of Diomedes during the seige of Troy

History:
1. 5th rate of 1803. Renamed *Africa* in 1859
2. Frigate of 1953
3. Corvette of 1877
4. Cruiser of 1901
5. Cruiser of 1939

Honours: Trafalgar 1805; Baltic 1854-55; Kagoshima 1863; Simonoseki 1864; Satsuma 1864; Egypt 1882; Heligoland 1914; Dardanelles 1915; Malta Convoys 1941-42; Mediterranean 1941-43; Sirte 1942; Sicily 1943; Salerno 1943; Okinawa 1945

Associations: 4th Bn Royal Regiment of Fusiliers (formed during the landing from *Euryalus* of the 1st Bn XX The Lancashire Fusiliers at Galipoli when the Battalion won six VCs 'before breakfast'); town of South Shields; 'Euryalus' PHAB centre, South Shields

Galatea

Name: A sea-nymph, daughter of Nereus and Doris

History:
1. 6th rate of 1776
2. 5th rate of 1794
3. 5th rate of 1810
4. Frigate of 1859
5. Cruiser of 1887
6. Cruiser of 1914. The first ship to sight the enemy at Jutland
7. Cruiser of 1934. Torpedoed in 1941
8. Name of the Humber Division of the RNVR, 1951

Honours: Penobscot 1779; Groix 1795; Tamatave 1811; Jutland 1916; Norway 1940; *Bismarck* action 1941; Mediterranean 1941

Associations: The city of Kingston upon Hull; various Hull charities

Hermione

Name: Daughter of Menelaus and Helen and wife of Orestes

History: Three ships of the same name were captured in 1757, 1759 and 1760 but probably none was added to the Navy
1. 5th rate of 1782. Carried by mutineers to La Guayra in 1797. Recaptured by boats of the *Surprise* in 1799 and renamed *Retaliation*, and later (1800) *Retribution*
2. Cruiser of 1893
3. Cruiser of 1939. Torpedoed in 1942

Honours: China 1900; *Bismarck* Action 1941; Mediterranean 1941; Malta Convoys 1941-42; Diego Suarez 1942

Associations: The town of Kendal; TS *Royalist*, Kendal (sea cadets); TS *Hermione*, Tidworth (sea cadets); Brooke House school, London

Juno

Name: The wife of Jupiter and Queen of Heaven, identified with the Greek Hera

History:
1. 5th rate of 1757. Burnt and abandoned at Rhode Island in 1778
2. 5th rate of 1780

3. 5th rate. Prize taken in 1809. Surrendered in 1809
4. 5th rate. Prize (*Bellone*) taken in 1810
5. 6th rate of 1844. Renamed *Atlanta* in 1878
6. Corvette of 1867
7. Cruiser of 1895
8. Destroyer of 1938. Sunk by aircraft in 1941

Honours: Louisburg 1758; Cuddalore 1783; Toulon 1793; Atlantic 1939; Calabria 1940; Libya 1940; Matapan 1941; Mediterranean 1940-41; Crete 1941; Malta Convoys 1941
Associations: The town of Eastbourne; Haydes School CCF; 5th Royal Inniskilling Dragoon Guards; 81st Tactical Fighter Wing USAF; Grange Road primary school, Gosport

Jupiter

Name: The supreme god of Heaven and earth, identified with the Greek Zeus
History:
1. 4th rate of 1778. Wrecked in 1808
2. 4th rate of 1813
3. Ex-*Porth*. Renamed 1863. Became a coal depot
4. Battleship of 1895
5. Destroyer of 1938
6. Name of the Reserve fleet in the Gareloch from 1950

Honours: Porto Praya 1781; Cape of Good Hope 1795; China 1839-42; Belgian Coast 1915-16; Mediterranean 1941; Malaya 1942
Associations: The town of Middlesbrough; TS *Jupiter*, Middlesbrough (sea cadets); TS *Valiant*, Barnstaple (sea cadets); Abbingdon junior school, Middlesbrough; Southlands school, Middlesbrough; The Green Howards

Leander

Name: Lover of Hero, who swam the Hellespont each night to visit her until he was drowned in a storm
History:
1. 4th rate of 1780. Surrendered to the *Genereux* in 1798. Recaptured by the Russians and Turks at Corfu in 1799 and restored by the Emperor of Russia. Renamed *Hygeia* in 1813
3. 4th rate of 1813
4. 4th rate of 1848
5. Cruiser of 1882
6. Cruiser of 1931

Honours: Tenerife 1797; Nile 1798; Algiers 1816; Black Sea 1854-55; Kula Gulf 1943
Associations: The town of Teignmouth, Devon; St George's School, Plymouth

Minerva

Name: The Roman goddess of wisdom, identified with the Greek Athena

History:
1. 5th rate of 1759. Surrendered in 1778 and retaken in 1781 when she was renamed *Recovery*
2. 5th rate of 1780. Renamed *Pallas* in 1798
5. 5th rate. Prize (*Minerve*) taken in 1795
7. 5th rate of 1805
9. 5th rate of 1820
10. Cruiser of 1895
15. Ex-*M33*, monitor of 1915. Converted to a minelayer and renamed in 1924. Later became a yard craft

Honours: Quiberon 1759; St Vincent 1797; Egypt 1801; Suez Canal 1915; Dardanelles 1915; Atlantic 1940; Falkland Islands 1982
Associations: Grindley's Bank of London; Ospringe primary school, Faversham, Kent; TS *St Kitts* (sea cadets); TS *Minerva* (sea cadets)

Naiad

Name: A freshwater nymph
History:
1. 5th rate of 1797
2. Cruiser of 1890
3. Cruiser of 1939. Torpedoed in 1942

A Belgian trawler, the *Naiade*, served in the RN 1916-19
Honours: Trafalgar 1805; Basque Roads 1809; Crete 1941; Mediterranean 1941; Malta Convoys 1942
Associations: The borough of Kingston upon Thames; The borough of Blackburn; Dunstable sea cadet corps; Steadfast sea cadet corps (Kingston upon Thames); The Queen's Own Hussars

Penelope

Name: The wife of Ulysses
History:
1. 6th rate of 1778. Foundered in 1779
2. 5th rate of 1783
4. 5th rate of 1798. Wrecked in 1815
5. 5th rate of 1829
6. Central battery ship of 1867 (she was the first large ironclad in the Navy to have twin screws)
7. Cruiser of 1914
8. Cruiser of 1935. Torpedoed in 1944

Honours: Egypt 1801; Martinique 1809; Baltic 1854; Alexandria 1882; South Africa 1899-1901; Norway 1940; Malta Convoys 1941-42; Mediterranean 1941-43; Sicily 1943; Sirte 1942; Aegean 1943; Salerno 1943; Anzio 1944; Falkland Islands 1982
Associations: The county borough of Blackpool; TS *Penelope*, Blackpool (sea cadets); TS *Radiant*, Dewsbury (sea cadets); Galworthy School for Autistic Children, Tavistock; Bankside Adult Education Centre, Chorley; Form 3c, Edge End high school, Nelson, Lancs

Phoebe

Name: A surname of Artemis as the Goddess of the moon
History:
1. 5th rate of 1795
2. 4th rate of 1854
4. Cruiser of 1890
5. Destroyer of 1916
7. Cruiser of 1939

Honours: Trafalgar 1805; Mauritius 1810; Java 1811; Benin 1897; Belgian Coast 1917-18; Zeebrugge 1918; Greece 1941; Crete 1941; Malta Convoys 1942; Aegean 1943; Mediterranean 1944; Sabang 1944; Burma 1944-45
Associations: The town of Bournemouth (started in 'ship adoption' week, 1942); TS *Phoebe*, Bournemouth (sea cadets); Summerbee secondary school, Bournemouth; Guide Dogs for the Blind Association

Scylla

Name: A monster inhabiting a rock in the Straits of Messina, which devoured the victims of the whirlpool Charybdis
History:
1. Sloop of 1809
2. Corvette of 1856
3. Cruiser of 1892
4. Cruiser of 1940

Honours: North Africa 1942; Arctic 1942-43; Salerno 1943; Atlantic 1943; Biscay 1943; Normandy 1944
Associations: The city of Aberdeen; TS *Scylla*, Aberdeen (sea cadets); Lynn Moor Home for Underprivileged Children, Aberdeen; TS *Brilliant*, Tunbridge Wells (sea cadets); Royal National Lifeboat Institution

Sirius

Name: The Dog Star
History:
1. 20 guns. Ex-*Berwick*, renamed in 1786. Wrecked in 1790
2. 5th rate of 1797. Destroyed to avoid capture in 1810
3. 5th rate of 1813. She was the last ship to be built at Bursledon
4. Sloop of 1868
5. Cruiser of 1890. Sunk as a blockship at Ostend in 1918
6. Cruiser of 1940

Honours: Calder's Action 1805; Trafalgar 1805; Belgian Coast 1914; Zeebrugge 1918; Arctic 1942; Malta Convoys 1942; Mediterranean 1942; North Africa 1942-43; Sicily 1943; Salerno 1943; Aegean 1943-44; Normandy

1944; South France 1944
Associations: The city of Portsmouth; TS *Sirius*, Hayes, Middlesex (sea cadets)

ROYAL AUSTRALIAN NAVY

Swan

Name: Originally named after the bird, now geographical
History:
1. Ballinger of 1417
5. 28 guns. Prize taken in 1636. Lost in 1638
6. 22 guns. Prize taken in 1652
10. 5th rate of 1673. Sunk by an earthquake at Jamaica in 1692
12. 6th rate of 1694. Foundered in 1707
13. 6th rate of 1709
14. Sloop of 1745
15. Sloop of 1767
23. Trawler during World War 1
24. Destroyer of 1916 built in Australia for the RAN, since when the name has remained the property of the RAN

Honours: Cadiz 1596; Gabbard 1653

Torrens

Name: Geographical. An Australian name, the current ship being the first bearer

ROYAL NETHERLANDS NAVY

Evertsen

Named after the Evertsen family, which suplied several admirals to the admiralty of Zealand. The 5th *Evertsen* was sunk in the Battle of the Java Sea. The 6th was purchased from the United Kingdom and took part in actions in Indonesia and Netherlands New Guinea. The present ship is the 7th to bear the name

Van Galen

Named after Lieutenant-Admiral Johan van Galen (1604-53). The 3rd *Van Galen* (a destroyer) took part in the defence of Rotterdam in May 1940 and was so severely damaged that it had to be abandoned. The ship sunk immediately afterwards. The present ship is the 5th of the name

Tjerk Hiddes

Named after Admiral Tjerk Hiddes de Vries, who distinguished himself during the period 1658-66, first as a captain of armed merchant vessels and later as a Flag Officer in the Four Days' Battle under de Ruyter. He was killed at the battle of Schooneveld. The 4th ship (ex-HMS *Non Pareil*) served in the RNIN from 1942-51 when it was transferred to the Indonesian navy and renamed *Gadjah Mada*. The present ship is the 5th of the name

Van Nes

Named after Lieutenant-Admiral Aert Jansz van Nes (1620-98). The 3rd ship of the name formed part of the Squadron under Rear Admiral Karel Doorman during the Japanese invasion of the Dutch East Indies. It went down fighting while protecting a convoy which evacuated soldiers from the islands of Banka and Billiton on 17 February 1942. The present ship is the 4th to bear the name

Van Speijk

Named after Lieutenant Jan Carel Josephus van Speijk, who, on 5 December 1831, as commanding officer of HM Gunboat No 2, set fire to the powder and was blown up with his ship when Belgians tried to overrun the gunboat during the blockade of Antwerp. The present ship is the 6th to bear the name, which by royal decree is borne in perpetuity by a ship of the RNIN

Isaac Sweers

Named after Vice-Admiral Isaac Sweers who was killed at the battle of Kijkduin on 23 August 1673.

The 2nd ship of the name was launched in March 1940 and, still incomplete, was towed to the UK in May. In company with two British destroyers in 1941 it sank two Italian cruisers in the Mediterranean. During the North Africa landings of 1942 it was torpedoed and sank with great loss of life. The current ship is the 3rd to bear the name

ROYAL NEW ZEALAND NAVY

Canterbury
Name: Geographical, originally in Britain, now the Province in New Zealand. The name dates from 1692
History:
2. 4th rate of 1693
4. Cruiser of 1915
Associations: The Province of Canterbury

Waikato
Name: Geographical. The present ship is the first to bear the name
Associations: The Province of Waikato

2 RN 'Leander' Modernisation

Ships	Batch I	Batch II	Batch III
	Leander	*Cleopatra*	*Andromeda*
	Naiad	*Phoebe*	*Jupiter*
	Euryalus	*Minerva*	*Hermione*
	Arethusa	*Argonaut*	*Bacchante*
	Ajax	*Sirius*	*Charybdis*
	Aurora	*Danae*	*Scylla*
	Galatea	*Juno* (1981)	*Achilles*
	Dido	*Penelope*	*Ariadne*
			Apollo
			Diomede
Radar and AIO	993 (*Naiad* 994) 1006, 1010, 1011 (*Leander*, *Ajax*, *Galatea*, all 944, 954M), Link 10 ADAWS 5	965Q (*Cleopatra* 996), 993, 1006, 1010, 1011, Link 10 (not *Juno*) CAAIS (not *Juno*) (*Juno* 978, 944M, 954M)	965Q (*Scylla, Jupiter, Hermione* all 965M) 978, 993, 944M, 954M
EW	UA9, 668, 669, Chaff	FH5 (not *Cleopatra, Phoebe, Minerva*, all UA13), UA8/9, 668 (not *Juno, Danae*, both 667)	FH5 (not *Hermione* FH4, *Ariadne, Apollo* both UA13), UA8/9, 668 (not *Hermione, Jupiter*, both 667) Chaff
Guns/Missiles/ Associated radars	Seacat/GWS22B/904 Two single 40/60	Exocet GWS50 (not *Juno*) Seacat GWS22C/D/904 Two single 40/60 (not *Juno*, two single 20mm, twin 4.5in Mk 6/MRS 3/ 903)	Twin 4.5in Mk 6 MRS3/ 903 One Seacat/GWS22/904 Two single 20mm (Sea Wolf in *Andromeda, Jupiter, Hermione*)

	Batch I	Batch II	Batch III
Sonar and AS weapons	162, 170, 182, 184M, 199, 185 (not *Ajax, Aurora, Euryalus, Naiad,* all 2008). Ikara/GWS41, Mortar Mk 10 Mod1, depth charges	162, 182, 184M (not *Juno* 177M), 185 (not *Danae, Cleopatra,* both 2008). Mk 44/46, depth charges, STWS (not *Juno,* Mortar Mk 10)	162, 170, 177, (*Apollo, Achilles, Diomede, Ariadne* all 184M), 185 (*Diomede* 2008), 199 (not *Scylla, Achilles, Diomede, Apollo, Ariadne*). Mortar Mk 10, Mk 44/46, depth charges
Aircraft	One Wasp	One Lynx (*Argonaut, Danae, Juno* one Wasp)	One Wasp

3 Missiles

ANTI-SUBMARINE (AS)

Ikara
Range: 15-18km
Dimensions: Length 3.43m, span 1.5m
Speed: Subsonic
Propulsion: Dual-thrust solid fuel
Control: Elevons
Guidance: Computer-based drop position updated during flight through autopilot and altimeter
Payload: Lightweight torpedo Mk 44 or Mk 46

SURFACE-TO-AIR (SAM)

Sea wolf
Range: 5km
Dimensions: Length 1.9m, span 56cm, diameter 18cm
Speed: M2+
Propulsion: Solid fuel 2-3sec burn
Control: Cruciform rear fins
Guidance: GWS25 — TV+target tracking Type 910 radar
Payload: 13.4kg warhead with impact and proximity fuze

Seacat
Range: 5km
Dimensions: Length 1.47m, span 65cm, diameter 19cm
Speed: M0.9
Propulsion: Dual-thrust solid fuel
Control: Cruciform rear fins
Guidance: GWS22/22B/22C — visual+target tracking Type 904 radar (TV autogathering in GWS24)
Payload: Blast warhead with proximity fuze

ANTI-SHIP (ASM)

Exocet
Range: Min 5-4km, max 42-45km
Dimensions: Length 5.21m, span 1.0m, diameter 34.8cm
Speed: M0.93
Propulsion: Boost — free-standing radially burning composite propellant, 2.4sec burn

Sustain — end-burning cast DB propellant, 93sec burn
Control: Cruciform rear fins
Guidance: Cruise — inertial+radio altimeter
Attack — X-band single axis radar seeker, search begins at 12-15km
Ship system — GWS50
Payload: 165kg blast/fragmentation hexolite warhead in steel block. Effective up to 70° incidence, delay+proximity fuze

Harpoon
Range: Max 110km
Dimensions: Length 4.58m, span 91.4cm, diameter 34.3cm
Speed: M0.85
Propulsion: Boost — 6,600kg composite propellant, 2.5sec burn, boosts to M0.75
Cruise — Teledyne CAE turbojet, 300kg thrust, endurance 15min
Control: Cruciform fins
Guidance: Cruise — inertial+radio altimeter
Attack — two-axis radar seeker
Payload: 227kg penetration blast, contact (with time delay)+proximity fuzes

Sea Skua
Range: 14km
Dimensions: Length 2.85m, span 62cm, diameter 22.2cm
Speed: Subsonic
Propulsion: Solid fuel
Control: Cruciform canard fins
Guidance: Semi-active radar homing
Payload: 35kg HE

AS12
Range: 6-800m
Dimensions: 187cm
Speed: Subsonic
Propulsion: Solid fuel
Control: Fins
Guidance: Wire
Payload: 29.7kg HE

4 Ballistic Weapons Systems

Bofors 40/60 Single Mounting
Calibre: 40mm
Length: 2.4m
M/V: 2,800ft/sec
Max elevation: 90°
Max range: Horizontal — 5 miles (10,750yd)
Vertical — 23,500ft
Fire control: Visual
Mounting: Open (with splinter shield)

Twin 4.5in Mk 6
Calibre: 114mm (4.5in)
Length: 5.1m
M/V: 2,350ft/sec (850m/sec)
Max elevation: 80°
Max range: Horizontal — 10 miles (20,000yd)

Vertical — 39,000ft
Rate of fire: 20 rounds/barrel/min
Projectile weight: 25kg
Fire control: MRS3/M20 series
Mounting: Armoured turret. Medium speed

Oto-Melara 76/62 Compact
Calibre: 76mm
Length: 4.7m
Max elevation: 85°
Rate of fire: 85 rounds/min
Fire control: M20 series
Mounting: Glass fibre compact mounting. High speed training and elevation

---

5 Data Handling Systems

System	Computer Outfit	Displays	Ships
ADAWS 5	DAE 1×FM1600 (64K words) (to be increased to 128K)	JZR 2 Plots 2 Totes 4 LPDs	Batch 1 Ikara *Leander* *Ajax* *Galatea* *Naiad* *Aurora* *Euryalus* *Arethusa* *Dido*
CAAIS	DBA(1) 1×FM1600B (32K words)	JHA(1)×6	Batch 2 Exocet *Cleopatra* *Phoebe* *Sirius* *Minerva* *Argonaut* *Danae* *Penelope* *Juno*
CAAIS	DBA(5) 1×FM1600B (48K words)	JHA(1)×6	Batch 3 *Andromeda* (GWS25) *Charybdis* *Hermione* *Jupiter* *Scylla* *Bacchante* *Achilles* *Diomede* *Apollo* *Ariadne*
DAISY 5	SMR (64K words)		*Van Speijk* (others of the class to follow)

6 Aircraft

Westland Wasp AS Mk1
Powerplant: One Bristol Siddeley Nimbus 503 turboshaft rated at 710shp
Performance: Max speed 120kt; cruising speed 110kt; max inclined climb rate 1,440ft/min; hovering climb (out of ground effect) 8,800ft; range 303 miles
Weight: Max take-off 5,500lb
Radar: Nil
Sonar: Nil
Crew: One pilot plus winchman for SAR/dispatch services
Dimensions: Rotor diameter 32ft 3in; fuselage length 30ft 5¾in; height 9ft 9in
Armament: Two AS torpedoes (Mk 44/46)/depth charges/AS12 ASM

Westland Lynx HAS MK2
Powerplant: Two Rolls-Royce 'Gem' BS360-07-26 turboshaft, each rated at 750shp (continuous), 900shp (max)
Performance: Max speed 145kt (one engine — 113kt); max inclined climb rate 2,020ft/min (one engine — 530ft/min); hovering ceiling 9,580ft; range 390 miles (with auxiliary fuel tanks — 650 miles)
Weight: 10,500lb max take-off
Radar: Ferranti Sea Spray
Sonar: Sonobuoys/Alcatel DUAV4
Crew: Pilot and observer plus winchman for SAR/dispatch services

Dimensions: Rotor diameter 42ft; fuselage length 39ft 1in (with rotor blades and tail folded — 34ft 10in); height 10ft 6in
Armament: Two AS torpedoes (Mk 44/46)/depth charges/Sea Skuas/AS12

Aerospatiale SA319B Alouette III
(Indian designation — **'Chetak'**)
Powerplant: One Astazou XIV turboshaft rated at 870shp
Performance: Max speed 118kt; cruising speed 106kt; max inclined rate of climb 885ft/min; hovering ceiling (out of ground effect) 5,575ft; range 375 miles
Weight: 4,960lb max take-off
Radar: Omera Orb 31
Sonar: Nil
Crew: One pilot plus winchman for SAR/dispatch services
Dimensions: Rotor diameter 36ft 1¾in; fuselage length 32ft 10¾in; height 9ft 10in
Armament: Two AS12/two Mk 44 AS torpedoes (one, with MAD)
Note: Weapons and sensor fits are frequently altered to suit national requirements of the moment and in the light of new developments

Below:
Charybdis on passage. *RN — Osprey*

7 Chronology

Name	Number	Laid Down	Launched	Commissioned	Modernised
Royal Navy					
Aurora	F10	1/6/61	28/11/62	9/4/64	3/76
Euryalus	F15	2/11/61	6/6/63	16/9/64	3/76
Galatea	F18	22/12/61	23/5/63	25/4/64	9/74
Arethusa	F38	7/9/62	5/11/63	24/11/65	4/77
Naiad	F39	30/10/62	4/11/63	15/3/65	7/75
Dido	F104	2/12/59	22/12/61	18/9/63	10/78
Leander	F109	10/4/59	28/6/61	27/3/63	12/72
Ajax	F114	12/10/59	16/8/62	10/12/63	9/73
Cleopatra	F28	19/6/63	25/3/64	4/1/66	11/75
Sirius	F40	9/8/63	22/9/64	15/6/66	10/77
Phoebe	F42	3/6/63	8/7/64	15/4/66	4/77
Minerva	F45	25/7/63	19/12/64	14/5/66	4/79
Danae	F47	16/12/64	31/10/65	7/9/67	9/80
Juno	F52	16/7/64	24/11/65	18/7/67	
Argonaut	F56	27/11/64	8/2/66	18/8/67	10/78
Penelope	F127	14/3/61	17/8/62	31/10/63	1/82
Achilles	F12	1/12/67	21/11/68	8/7/70	
Diomede	F16	30/1/68	15/4/69	2/4/71	
Andromeda	F57	25/4/66	24/5/67	2/12/68	12/80
Hermione	F58	6/12/65	26/4/67	11/7/69	3/83
Jupiter	F60	3/10/66	4/9/67	2/8/69	7/83
Bacchante	F69	27/10/66	29/2/68	17/10/69	
Apollo	F70	1/5/69	15/10/70	28/5/72	
Scylla	F71	17/5/69	8/8/68	12/2/70	9/83
Ariadne	F72	1/11/69	10/9/71	10/2/73	
Charybdis	F75	27/1/67	28/2/68	2/6/69	6/82
Royal Australian Navy					
Swan	D50	18/8/65	16/12/67	20/1/70	/84
Torrens	D53	18/8/65	28/9/68	19/1/71	/84
Royal New Zealand Navy					
Waikato	F55	10/1/64	18/2/65	12/9/66	
Canterbury	F421	12/4/69	6/5/70	22/10/71	
Royal Netherlands Navy					
Van Speijk	F802	1/10/63	5/3/65	14/2/67	
Van Galen	F803	25/7/63	19/6/65	1/3/67	
Tjerk Hiddes	F804	1/6/64	17/12/65	16/8/67	
Van Nes	F805	25/7/63	26/3/66	9/8/67	
Isaac Sweers	F814	5/5/65	10/3/67	15/5/68	
Evertsen	F815	6/7/65	18/6/66	21/12/67	
Indian Navy					
Himgiri	F34	/67	6/5/70	23/11/75	
Nilgiri	F33	/10/66	23/10/68	3/6/72	
Udaygiri	F35	/1/73	9/3/74	1/2/77	
Dunagiri	F36	14/9/70	24/10/72	18/2/76	
Taragiri	F41	/74	25/10/76	/79	
Vindhyagiri	F38	/75	12/11/77	/79	
Chilean Navy					
Condell	06	5/6/71	12/6/72	21/12/73	
Almirante Lynch	07	6/12/71	6/12/72	22/5/74	